"*Imprisoned to Hope* weaves personal story with poetry and the ancient wisdom of the Scriptures to paint a picture of the possibility of forgiveness in a broken world. If you have experienced tragedy, disillusionment, or heartbreak, then this book will guide you through your pain to a place of wholeness where you can become a voice of hope for others."

—**Steve Knox**,
Founder of Orbiting Normal,
Author of *The Asymmetrical Leader*

"You would think that Christians would be experts in forgiveness, not only because we've been forgiven much but also because we're commanded by Christ to forgive others. But unforgiveness is a perennial problem in the Church. Why? Enter Vernon Burger's insightful study on the importance of lament. Based on his careful study of the Scriptures, Burger describes what he calls the "anatomy of lament," that which is constitutive of genuine, liberating, revolutionary forgiveness. Since we don't know how to truly grieve over our sin—not only our personal foibles but also the injustices of the world—we fail to realize the forgiveness only Christ can bring. Punctuated by his own story of abuse and restless longing for healing, Burger explains how a wounded soul finds restoration in the singular act of biblical lamentation *in Christ*. A must-read for those who identify with Jesus's lament on the cross, 'My God, my God, why have you forsaken me?'"

—**Rodney Reeves**,
Dean and Redford Professor of Biblical Studies,
Southwest Baptist University

"Vernon Burger is intelligent. His candor, thought processes, and insight to an underdeveloped piece of Christian theology is brilliant. The reflective insight and personal strength afforded to the reader from the life of Vernon is on point. Sit back. Put on your thinking cap and enjoy the power of knowing the Father in heaven in a whole new way."

—**Jerrell Altic**,
Minister of Mobilization,
Prayer, Missions, and Connection Center,
Houston's First Baptist Church,
Houston, Texas

"With the raw emotions that come with lament, Vernon Burger charts a course back home from the dark places of pain. *Imprisoned to Hope* is the spiritual journey that so many people need to see how God meets us in our pain and delivers us into a closer relationship with Christ."

—**Dr. Philip Nation**,
Pastor, Author of *Habits for Our Holiness*

"Hope-filled lament seems like a contradictory term, but it is not—nor should it be! Vernon Burger's uniquely insightful and vulnerable book Imprisoned to Hope reminds us that truly following Jesus also means walking with Him into difficult days, darkness, and disappointment—but with the abiding promises of hope firmly attached. The full council of God's Word is replete with stories, sagas, and songs of lament and sorrow; therefore, tears and hurt must surely be a part of a Christian's journey and experience. But as Vernon points out, we tend to want to quickly rush through seasons of sorrow and days of pain. It is often at the confluence of sadness, betrayal, confusion, and heaviness that God's lifting grace is most clearly realized. I highly recommend this biblically-rich book to anyone who has wondered where weeping and hope intersect, and how the Glory of God expands and the good of His own children benefit from discovering and practicing lamentation."

—**John Durham**,
Lead Pastor, Highland Baptist Church, Waco, Texas

"It's so rare to see a book on this subject, but it is beyond necessary and long overdue. This great work will lead you to a healthy perspective of worship in hardship, maybe for the first time."

—**Tedashii Anderson**,
Artist/Performer, Radio Host, Speaker, Writer

"Vernon is a tour guide in the truest sense of the word. He walks us gently through the twists and turns of violent valleys no one plans for their life. Unfortunately, life forces us to face hardships. With his own story of pain and promise, Vernon not only teaches us to trust God through tragedy, he teaches us to trust God with tragedy. Take the journey ahead and you will begin to hear healing and find hope through the power of lament. God's unparalleled grace and mercy are woven like a tapestry through the pages you hold in your hands. Read and find freedom."

—Jeremy Foster,
Pastor, Hope City Church, Houston, Texas

The American church does not understand lamentation and does not like to lament. The unwise aversion to lament has contributed to the thinness of American Christianity. With *Imprisoned to Hope* Vernon Burger has sent up a signal flare and alerted us to the loss we suffer when we refuse the necessary role of lament. In this well-researched and well-written book, Burger traces lament through the Bible and insightfully connects it with the practice of Christian forgiveness. *Imprisoned to Hope* offers a pathway toward healing that many of us need to walk.

—Brian Zahnd
Pastor of Word of Life Church, St. Joseph, Missouri,
Author of *Sinners in the Hands of a Loving God*

IMPRISONED TO HOPE

FORGIVENESS AS A FORM OF LAMENT

VERNON BURGER II

LUCIDBOOKS

Imprisoned to Hope: Forgiveness as a Form of Lament

Published by Lucid Books in Houston, TX.
www.LucidBooksPublishing.com

First Printing 2017

eISBN 10: 1632961326
eISBN 13: 9781632961327
ISBN 10: 1632961318
ISBN 13: 9781632961310

Special Sales: Most Lucid Books titles are available in special quantity discounts. Custom imprinting or excerpting can also be done to fit special needs. Contact Lucid Books at info@lucidbookspublishing.com.

To Amber, Titus, and Justus.
You are a gift beyond what can be expressed in words.
Live loved.
Live the questions.

A Note to the Reader

This work is an adaptation of my doctoral dissertation. I have attempted to take out some of the technical language that I used for the academy, while also incorporating some of my own personal story. Honestly, this has proven more difficult than I had ever imagined. I hadn't originally planned on exercising so much personal vulnerability with my own story, and I've edited out nearly half the length of my dissertation. Both have been rewarding, but hard, work.

All of the proceeds from this book will go to His Voice Global. My goal is for people to not only experience personal healing through this work, but also to know their purchase has helped many other people around the world from South Sudan to Kenya to India. With that said, thank you so much for helping those who you may never meet this side of Heaven, but know you have helped to influence their lives.

Table of Contents

Preface

Life Snapshot #1

My sister and I were just sitting on the couch. Suddenly, we saw a Dr. Scholl's wooden sandal fly through the air towards my dad's head. We were in the throes of yet another argument. Once again, my dad had calmly said something insulting, and my mom had lost it emotionally. The argument quickly escalated to become physical, and before we knew it, my dad was pushing my mom into the entertainment center.

Less than a week later, both of my parents were at my little league game. My dad helped coach the team while my mom sat in the stands cheering us on—a perfect picture of happy, domestic life. This unsteady, unpredictable violence and then love, brokenness and then safety, war and then peace, is what our life was as we grew up. Internally, I was begging for compassion from my parents, but the reality of life was that I was constantly on high alert, trying to anticipate the next emotional explosion.

My story is one of brokenness—a story many know all

too well. And yet, as a believer in Jesus, I know broken and strained relationships are not the final word. Our lives can be shattered in many ways, but I believe the Bible teaches our brokenness is not beyond repair. The biblical account gives a picture of a beautiful beginning that is eventually deeply marred by sin and evil, yet the picture is one that culminates in our wounds becoming scars.

Life Snapshot #2

As I held her warm hand, her life was slipping away. The cold room was filled with the sacred fire of transition. Mom was drawing her last breath. My sister and I looked at her body as it gave way and her spirit was swallowed up with more life. Jesus held her. Jesus holds her.

We didn't feel like we could cry anymore. Our mom's last week alive was filled with more tears and laughter, angst and comfort, clarity and chaos, than we could articulate today. Though it's hard to put into words, that last week was a perfect microcosm of what it felt like growing up.

Mom was bipolar and our household looked like this, in all of its pain and joy. One day, I could come home and she would be the most loving and caring person. Then, within a matter of moments, our world would come crashing down with a piercingly degrading comment, or some form of humiliating physical or sexual abuse—and sometimes we were just ignored.

Growing up felt much like getting caught in a tornado. Sometimes we could clearly see the tornado coming and we could expect when we'd be thrown into the air by the rushing winds. Other times the tornado would just blindside us.

Uncertainty was certain. We didn't know if we'd be met with a smile or scowl within a given hour.

This type of uncertainty may be the reason I have longed for structure and stability later in life. Maybe structure is just hardwired into me. Maybe it's both. Either way, growing up in this type of environment, filled with extreme highs and extreme lows, led to a life that felt like perpetual disorientation. It is from this deep disorientation I came to eventually know Jesus when I was nineteen. Unfortunately, what I found in much of the faith community was not a place where I could take my pain, doubts, and questions. Many of the built-in answers in that community were to learn how to turn the pain to praise, doubts to certainties, and questions to simple answers. In other words, I didn't have a language of honesty when it came to the pains and disappointments of life.

The more I grew in faith and read the Scriptures, though, the more I became well acquainted with pain and sorrow. The groans of Paul, the doubts of Job and Jeremiah. The poetic questions and angst of the Psalms, along with the cries of Jesus. You see, the God of the Scriptures speaks a language of hope, but He also accepts—even encourages—our lament! He is as near to us in the midst of darkness as He is during times of light. He is not only the God of both light and dark, but He is God with Us (Immanuel) in both. When we learn to adopt the hope of lament, we not only learn how to vocalize our deepest violations, but we also learn how to walk in the victorious lifestyle of forgiveness towards ourselves and others.

There's a need for more books on the subject of suffering, doubt, and lament. What I want to explore is the need to connect lament as a viable form of worship and see how lament is foundationally interlocked with forgiveness. But my exploration isn't simply a cerebral exercise. I was raised in a home that can be characterized as "walking on eggshells." I do not doubt my parents had a deep love for my sister and me, but the reality is that we both experienced an excruciating amount of abuse.

I have also started a nonprofit that is associated with deep pains of loss and mourning. At His Voice Global, we have walked with many hurting people. Children who have lost parents, widows who have lost their husbands, and church leaders who are leading in profound ways of reconciliation among those who have been violated in the deepest ways imaginable.

There is great hope in the middle of devastation, but this must not come at a price of overlooking difficulty or sweeping the painful realities of life under the rug. With all of this in mind, *Imprisoned to Hope* is my attempt to give voice to the desperate need for recovering lament as a viable form of expressing faith, especially when it comes to forgiveness.

Introduction

As we take this journey together, I will tell my own personal story of pain, abuse, confusion, and struggle, and the ongoing process of redemption. Along the way, we'll discover together what the Bible has to say about these things. How we can address issues of abuse, pain and disappointment, and how we can begin to embrace forgiving others who have harmed us.

One thing I have continually learned is that many people consider lament to be a "second-class citizen" to praise, when it comes to their faith walk. But suffering crosses cultural divides. It is not just among the destitute we have served alongside of in South Sudan, Kenya, and India. Suffering also exists among the rich and well-off in America. Suffering, pain, and violation cross all social classes, whether someone cannot afford the next meal or they have five cars and a mansion. Often, a suffering person's inability to see God's presence in the midst of darkness is one of the greatest reasons many abandon faith in the God of the Bible.

Chapter Overviews

In the first chapter, we'll explore the overall Metanarrative of the Bible to get a wide scope on how forgiveness as lament fits into the Bible's "Big Story." We'll look through the lens of three different snapshots (although many different snapshots exist). These snapshots are what I call The Unified Story, The Disunified Story, and The Reunified Story. We'll explore each "story" in order to see forgiveness as lament in its overall place in the entire Meta-Story.

In the second chapter, we'll discover the foundations of lament, along with the anatomy of lament. Lament needs to be recovered as a common form of worship in our expression of our Christian faith. I'll also begin to make the case for how lament is essential if forgiveness is ever to be granted to another.

In the third chapter, we will explore the Old Testament Psalms. Since the Psalms are broken up into five books, we will explore one psalm from each book. Then we will begin to unpack the anatomy of lament and I'll outline it as violation, vocalization, and victory.

In the fourth chapter, I will discuss forgiveness as lament for humanity. I will define forgiveness, and we'll take a look at the anatomy of forgiveness in much the same way as we approached the anatomy of lament. The reality is that, when an offense against us is not taken seriously enough, when we're unable to express anger towards our situations of violation and pain, then forgiveness can never be truly granted to the other. But when we can move through these markers of lament and truly become grieved and angered by them, then we're able to live life in honesty without becoming hateful.

When we are violated in some way, feeling and expressing anger is appropriate, but we will also learn that anger doesn't need to have the final word when forgiveness becomes an option.

In the fifth chapter, I make the argument that God forgives by lamenting. We'll look into questions such as "Was Jesus abandoned on the Cross?" After this, I make the case that there exists within the Trinity a solidarity of lament. This solidarity is foundational to our ability to offer forgiveness to others.

In the sixth chapter, we will trace lament through the New Testament and concentrate on the third part of the stated anatomy, which is victory. What does true victory actually look like in lament? We'll look for a path forward that is faithful to the human experience and what Scripture teaches.

In the seventh chapter, we'll dive into what could be considered enemies and allies of forgiveness as a lament. We'll explore denial versus acceptance, violence versus new possibility, personal control versus God's sovereignty, busyness versus sabbath, and silence versus vocalizing. Although this is not an exhaustive list by any means, it gives a strong basis for paving the road to see how forgiveness as lament is a viable alternative.

Finally, in the eighth chapter, we will bring the previous seven chapters together by seeing how we can actually not only see how forgiveness is a lament, but also how we can implement this in our lives.

Before we begin, consider the brilliant twentieth-century poet T.S. Eliot, who gave us the gift of a vision of hope in exploring the topic of lament and forgiveness in his poem "Little Gidding" from *Four Quartets.*

We shall not cease from exploration
And the end of all our exploring
Will be to arrive where we started
And know the place for the first time.[1]

May seeing forgiveness as a lament offer a way for us to arrive where we first started in being reconciled to God. In our reconciliation, we recognize, possibly for the first time, that a Suffering God provides a path ahead. A path large enough to see that authentic faith doesn't only involve praise and thanksgiving, but also tears, cries, and questions.

CHAPTER 1

The Grand Story

The Grand Story

Do you ever have days, weeks, or years in your life when you ask yourself, "How did this all happen?" We all live with disappointments, trials, and even tragedies in life. How did God's original design get so marred by sin, and why is it that a life of peace, joy, love, and acceptance seems just out of our reach? Is there any way to understand what in the world is going on? Can the Bible give us any help?

As we ask these questions, our work going forward in this book is to look at the overarching, foundational Big Picture of the Bible. When we can get our "Big Picture" view of life from the narrative of the Bible, it allows us to see how lament is found throughout the story of Scripture, and how the way of forgiveness as lament offers a picture that is faithful to the main storyline of the Bible. Understanding lament and forgiveness, along with how the two go hand-in-hand, is critical to understanding how to live a life of faith with God, others, and the rest of creation.

In this chapter, we'll discuss the themes of biblical Metanarrative much the same way as we'd think about three major acts, as in a play. We all have stories and live according to story. Act One of the biblical Big Story is what we call a "Unified" story. We'll look at pre-creation and creation, along with the relationships between God, humankind, and nonhuman creation.

Of course we know that in the "Fall" of humankind in Genesis 3, humankind became "Disunified." This is Act 2. The chaos that ensued between God, mankind, and nonhuman creation resulted in the breaking of unity. This is where lament gets introduced into the big picture.

Act Three ("Reunification") shows a picture of how Jesus and His life are the foundational focus for seeing the way in which the Triune God chooses to reunify God, man, and nonhuman creation. This happens at the pivotal point of the Cross of Jesus Christ where Father, Son, and Holy Spirit stay in perfect unity, and provides a way forward for reunification in forgiveness through lament.

All good stories have a general arc like this—an arc that includes unity, disunity, and finally reunification. We long for reconciliation and restoration when disunity has abounded, yet the way forward is not to have an irrational optimism. The way to learn how to honestly engage in disunity is by learning how to adopt the hope of lament and the possibility for honest reunification. Unfortunately, many professing Christians adopt an unhealthy view of suffering that wants to "sweep it under the rug." In these kinds of situations, sadly, lament is seen as the antithesis of faith, instead of an expression of it.

Unified

Before creation, there was unified community and contented relationship between the Father, Son, and Holy Spirit. As Thomas McCall says, "God [doesn't] need us . . . the triune God knows no lack or need. The expression of His grace toward us is, then, completely free. God does not love us out of a lack or emptiness; instead, He loves us out of the fullness of the triune life of holy love."[1] The ultimate essence of life must be understood through this lens of unified relationship. The creative expression of unity in the Trinity gives birth to creation, and gives mankind a way to understand how God calls every aspect of the created order to live in harmonious relationship.

The Creation Story of Genesis 1 and 2 should be understood as the expression of the Triune God's relational creativity. It is the artistry of unity at its finest.

Colossians 1:17 tells us it was Jesus who spoke Creation into existence: "For by Him all things were created, in heaven and on earth, visible and invisible, whether thrones or dominions or rulers or authorities—all things were created through Him and for Him." Yet the Creation Story also involves the Holy Spirit and the Father, who are also a part of the act according to Genesis 1:2: "The earth was without form and void, and darkness was over the face of the deep. And the Spirit of God was hovering over the face of the waters." It is this artistic community of the Trinity that gives expression and form to the stars and trees and animals and ocean and humanity.

In Genesis 1–2, we see the "God-breathed" creative beauty of creation was in perfect harmony. The Bible calls this "*shalom.*" *Shalom* is the idea that everything is operating as it should, and is in perfect harmony with every other part of the created order. The plant and animal kingdoms, along with humankind, lived in perfect *shalom* at the beginning of Creation, all expressing their unique roles according to creation in perfect unity with one another.

Yet the perfect harmony of loving stewardship came to a crashing fracture because man decided his position was not good enough. Instead, he began to believe the lie that imaging God was a second-rate position, and he decided he needed to *be* God. Disunity broke in and wreaked havoc not only on humanity, but on the entire created order. Domineering took the place of loving stewardship, and every square inch of the created order felt the shocking reverberations of this fractured unity.

Some have experienced this disunity as I have talked about in my experience growing up, while others have experienced this type of domineering in a variety of other ways. Some form codependent relationships, either to church leaders who are on ego trips (often along the lines of "God gave me a vision") or to judgmental spouses. Disunity wreaks so much havoc precisely because we were built to be in unity, in *shalom.*

Disunified

Before the Fall of Man in Genesis 3, the Fall of Satan occurred (see Luke 10:18). Sometime after this first Fall, Satan came to the garden to tempt Eve. The only way this temptation could have happened was if Satan had already broken communion with the Trinity. Here is how the Bible tells this story:

> Now the serpent was more crafty than any other beast of the field that the LORD God had made. He said to the woman, "Did God actually say, 'You shall not eat of any tree in the garden'?" And the woman said to the serpent, "We may eat of the fruit of the trees in the garden, but God said, 'You shall not eat of the fruit of the tree that is in the midst of the garden, neither shall you touch it, lest you die.'" But the serpent said to the woman, "You will not surely die. For God knows that when you eat of it your eyes will be opened, and you will be like God, knowing good and evil."
>
> —Gen. 3:1–5

Adam and Eve followed Satan's invitation to eat from the only tree in the garden God said not to partake of. The immediate result of breaking the relationship with God was shame: "Then the eyes of both were opened, and they knew that they were naked. And they sewed fig leaves together and made themselves loincloths" (Gen. 3:7).

This "hiddenness" is the root of sin. Adam and Eve express externally (through hiding) what was happening internally. Hiding can happen in one of two ways: either prideful self-exaltation, or shameful self-deprecation. When we either make "too much" or "too little" of ourselves, instead of having a proper assessment of ourselves, we hide from who we truly are.

In my own story, I have found this dynamic to be prevalent. I often would set out to prove myself and show my parents I was good enough. In my pride, I would set out to show them that I could overcome odds and be good at something like sports. On the other hand, I simultaneously had incredibly low self-esteem. I would beat myself up and continually, saying I was never good at anything. The first moments of what I felt to be failure made me jump into a fortress of self-protection. As Paul Tripp has said on many different occasions, "Many times we respond sinfully to being sinned against." Sure, my parents should not have done some of the things they did to me. There is no excuse. Yet I shouldn't have sinned, either. There is no excuse.

Prideful self-exaltation has dozens of examples in the Scriptures, and we'll explore a couple. A prime example of self-exaltation is the story of Cain and Abel in Genesis 4, shortly after the fall. This story documents how God spoke with Cain and warned him, "If you do well, will you not be accepted? And if you do not do well, sin is crouching at your door. Its desire is for you, but you must rule over it." Yet Cain decides not to believe God and kills Abel instead.[2]

Fast-forward to the New Testament, and we see an example of hiding through prideful self-exaltation in the lives of the Pharisees. Jesus constantly criticizes all the ways in which they continually lifted themselves above others, but the best summation is found in "The Seven Woes" He articulates in Matthew 23:11–36.

The Pharisees' pride of wanting recognition for godliness is the complete antithesis of grace, because humanity is already fully known by God. There's no earning salvation. Hiding behind religious works leads to comparing ourselves to others, which is a form of coveting. The result of our coveting is disunity with God and with others. Self-exaltation always results in the desire to draw people to ourselves, instead of showing them the grace of God for those who believe He is the Great Unifier.

Yet shameful self-deprecation is another way many people hide. The story of Saul in the Old Testament is an instance of this: Saul is appointed as the first king of Israel and is the most powerful man among his people, but his personal insecurities drive him mad, literally. David comes to play the harp for Saul in order to assuage his fits, and Saul repays him by trying to kill him. Saul doesn't wait on or listen to the Lord, and he makes many attempts to kill David. Then Samuel comes to Saul and diagnoses all the reasons for his erratic, insecure, and sinful actions by saying, "Though you are little in your own eyes, are you not the head of the tribes of Israel? The LORD anointed you king over Israel" (1 Sam. 15:17). Everything Saul did came from a place of self-deprecation. Nothing was ever enough for him. Instead of living openly with God, he chose to hide behind his insecurities, which ultimately manifested itself in his ongoing pursuit to kill David.

Prideful self-exaltation and shameful self-deprecation best describe the inherent chaos of disunity. Ultimately, when we try to become the centers of our own worlds, either by making too much or too little of ourselves, we hide. Yet even in the face of such disunity, this is not what has the last word. It's not the last word in the Big Story or in our own personal life stories. The God of the Bible sets out a picture of grace that is set on reunifying a broken world and healing it in such a way that *shalom* can be seen and known to all. In view of this, it is time to see the picture of reunification. When we're able to be reunified with God and others, lament can then be set properly in the overall Metanarrative. Only then can forgiveness as a form of lament be seen as a way toward hope.

Reunified

Shame arose because Adam and Eve chose to hide. Yet the act of God's reunification starts quickly in Scripture. Right after God tells the Serpent, Adam, and Eve the curse for disobedience, we read this in Genesis 3:21–24:

> And the LORD God made for Adam and for his wife garments of skins and clothed them. Then the LORD God said, "Behold, the man has become like one of us in knowing good and evil. Now, lest he reach out his hand and take also of the tree of life and eat, and live forever—" Therefore the LORD God sent him out from the garden of Eden to work the ground from which he was taken. He drove out the man, and at the east of the garden of Eden he placed the cherubim and a flaming sword that turned every way to guard the way to the tree of life."

God doesn't tell them they'll never be able to be back in relationship, and He doesn't say they need to earn their way back. God initiates. Instead, God introduces the idea of reunification through grace by making garments for Adam and Eve to wear.

After making Adam and Eve clothes, God sends them out of the Garden of Eden. At first, this may seem like the antithesis of reunification, but look at the way God expresses his love. Adam and Eve decided to "ingest death" by eating from the tree of knowing good and evil. Consider the logic behind the banishment from Eden: If they kept "ingesting death," and then ate from the tree of life, they would have experienced living death forever. Instead, God sets up the boundary from Eden. God disciplines those He loves, because they're His children.

Although it is a bit unfair to try and make a broad brush-stroke of the entire Old Testament, the general arc is that God's people continually rebel against who they ultimately are. God's people are to live as loved children of God. Instead, they run away. They hide. Yet God graciously pursues, so they can be reunified through merciful love.

The Good News of the Bible can be summarized as God bringing everything under His loving rule through the Spirit-filled life, teaching, death, resurrection, ascension, intercession, and second coming of Jesus Christ. It is not inherently just the Cross and resurrection that bring the ability for reunification through forgiveness. After all, plenty of people died on a cross before Jesus, and people were raised from the dead before Jesus. It is a matter of seeing the totality of all of Jesus's existence as the essence of why and how reunification is possible.

The loving rule of God (His Kingdom) is ushered in through the incarnation. Jesus took on flesh and came to the world. The incarnation is also the perfect picture of mercy. Mercy is best understood as entering into pain and offering healing from the inside out. The inside of pain. The inside of brokenness. The inside of shame. He renovates, not by simply "glossing over" our troubles, but instead, He enters into the deepest parts of our devastation and offers deep healing.

It is like a stained glass window. Our lives are many different colors, and they can be shattered at times. Yet the Merciful One picks up the shattered (yet still sacred!) colors of glass, binds them together again, and makes a brilliant work of art, not in spite of the "darker colors," but with them.

This is exactly what Jesus came to do! He entered into the pain of the world, its disunity, and offered healing from the inside out. The Kingdom of God began when Mary became pregnant with Jesus. When He came to Earth, He led the way for all of creation to follow in the Exodus of the New Creation. It is a march of hope. A march to the renewal of all things. A march that will be paved through His life and death that offers forgiveness of sin and fullness of life.

It is also the teaching of Jesus that is part of the Good News and paints the picture of The Kingdom of mercy. He comes to teach, not only in words, but also in actions. He heals the sick, resurrects the dead, and casts out demons. He enters into the chaos and disunity in order to bring about reunification and healing to the world. Yet it is not only healing to humanity, it is also to the rest of nonhuman creation.

One example is in Luke 8:22–26, when Jesus calms the sea as it rages out of control during a storm. The sea is known as a picture of chaos to the people. Therefore, it is not simply Jesus saving his disciples from a storm. He is also showing that He brings nonhuman creation from disunity to reunity, from chaos to order—and that He is Lord of all creation.

Another example is the Cross, which is the fulcrum point of history, whereby The Spirit-filled Merciful One offers up loud cries and laments during his death. In his death, He shows that communion was never broken in the Trinity. Instead, the Trinity entered into the most profound depths of the pain of sin and Jesus gave the opportunity for the reunification of all creation with God through his faithful Spirit-filled tears.

When Jesus went to the cross and was crucified, He not

only conquered death, He set creation on a path for healing. After all, the killing of cancer does not inherently mean someone is healed. The eradication of cancer cells simply sets the environment for the possibility of building the body back up to full health. The death of death allows for the flourishing of life.

The way Peter says this is, "He himself bore our sins in his body on the tree, that we might die to sin and live to righteousness. By his wounds you have been healed." (1 Pet. 2:24). Through the wounds of Jesus on the Cross and the Spirit breathing life, resurrection speaks an anthem. An anthem of sin conquered and the world being filled with life! In 1 Corinthians 15:54–55, Paul paints a powerful picture of resurrection: "Death is swallowed up in victory. O death, where is your victory? O death where is your sting?"

Even before his death occurs, Jesus gives insight into the focus of resurrection in John 11:25–26. He says, "I am the resurrection and the life. Whoever believes in me, though he die, yet shall he live, and everyone who lives and believes in me shall never die." The resurrection is focused on Jesus, and resurrection comes from Jesus, "For by him all things were created, in heaven and on earth, visible and invisible, whether thrones or dominions or rulers or authorities—all things were created through him and for him . . . For in him all the fullness of God was pleased to dwell" (Col. 1:16–17, 19). The reunification of the world is found in the relational reconciliation that a Spirit-filled, Father-focused Jesus offers. As Bartholomew and Goheen said, "In his resurrection, Jesus opens the door to the new creation—and then holds that door open and invites us to join Him."[3]

Yet The Good News does not stop with the resurrection.

Jesus also ascended to Heaven (Luke 24:50–53). It is important to consider and visualize this for multiple reasons. First of all, His ascension is a picture of Jesus reigning right now. It is not simply a future rule that happens when He comes back a second time. He is currently King.

Next, Jesus ascends bodily. It is a picture that means Christianity is not just about "the unseen." Christians are not neo-platonic, believing that only the unseen is good and the physical is bad. Instead, Christianity believes the unseen and the physical world are good. In other words, matter matters, as has been said by many throughout history. The current King is in flesh and blood as a picture of the final state of humanity not as disembodied spirits, but as having flesh and blood uncorrupted by sin. Paul says in 2 Corinthians 5:4–5, "For while we are still in this tent, we groan, being burdened—not that we would be unclothed, but that we would be further clothed, so that what is mortal may be swallowed up by life. He who has prepared us for this very thing is God, who has given us the Spirit as a guarantee." The ultimate end is to be "further clothed" by being "swallowed up by life"—the same life that was strong enough to swallow up death, sin, and the grave. The Ascended King ushers in His Kingdom by renewing humanity, earth, and the entire cosmos.

Finally, the Second Coming of the Spirit-filled, Father-focused Jesus is the culmination of the Good News of God, who brings everything under His loving rule. The Second Coming is the consummation of the Kingdom inaugurated by Jesus. Properly understood, this is when Heaven comes down to Earth and all things are made new. Yet, this newness is not something that is a completely "other" creation.

It is this creation, both human and nonhuman, that is fully restored.

Revelation 21:1–4 records it this way:

> Then I saw a new heaven and a new earth, for the first heaven and the first earth had passed away, and the sea was no more. And I saw the holy city, new Jerusalem, coming down out of heaven from God, prepared as a bride adorned for her husband. And I heard a loud voice from the throne saying, "Behold, the dwelling place of God is with man. He will dwell with them, and they will be his people, and God himself will be with them as their God. He will wipe away every tear from their eyes, and death shall be no more, neither shall there be mourning, nor crying, nor pain anymore, for the former things have passed away."

This is the time in which all the tears of suffering are wiped away and will be no more. The reasons for these tears are many, and represent lament in all its forms of betrayal and violation. In view of Revelation 21, it is understood that tears being wiped away predicates the truth that tears exist.

In my own story, I have experienced each of the themes we have explored in this chapter, and maybe you have, too. We all have a picture of *shalom*—holistic flourishing, the good life. Growing up, I had moments of this in my life, but it never lasted. It almost felt like having a drink of cold soda in the middle of a hot day. It refreshes for a moment, but if you do not have real water, it feels like you are worse off five minutes from the time you drank the soda.

This is the type of disunity that was present in my family

story. Your family story may be much different from mine, but we all experience brokenness to some degree. Yet this is not the end of the story. God met me and reunified me to Himself. It is my hope you meet God in this way as well. All the pain has not been swept away yet, but know that He listens to your cries. He knows your pain and anger, and one day will wipe away every tear. To this end, let's turn to exploring the need to recover a vital expression of faith: lament.

CHAPTER 2

The Foundation and Anatomy of Lament

Sometimes we can think of complaint as evidence of weak or nonexistent faith. When I came to faith in Jesus, I thought the only proper way to talk with God was to make sure everything was "wrapped up in praise." It came out with language like, "Well, you know, everything works out for the good." Or, "Well, even though this is tough, to God be the glory." I had this idea that having it together was the point of Christianity. In all of it, I must confess, I remained the center of my narrative. God was small. My praise was big. I needed everyone to see my strength. Ultimately, I was being dishonest, yet I received the praise of many.

Thankfully, Scripture gives a different picture. We can learn to be honest with both our praise and our pain. The path forward in the middle of our darkness is a type of worship the Bible calls lament. Lament is properly understood as *complaint that finds its trust in God.* Lament is something that is present through the entire corpus of Scripture.

> We tend to think of the laments primarily in relation to the Psalms and Job and Lamentations. That is where they are especially lodged. But theologically, the cry to God and the response of God are a fundamental theme of the whole of Scripture. The human cry to God for help is not one element in the biblical story; it is one of its foundation stones, foundational for both our anthropology and our theology.[1]

Moses laments that he cannot speak (Ex. 4:10), although God says he is the one to be the mouthpiece for delivering the people. When God calls Gideon, he laments that his clan is the weakest in Manasseh and that he is the least in his family (Judg. 6:15). When Isaiah encounters the holiness of God, he responds with a lament. Jeremiah continues the tapestry of lament by responding to God's commissioning of him by saying he is too young and cannot speak (Jer. 1:6). Yet the Lord responds simply by saying that His presence is sufficient. Ezekiel was commissioned with a message of lament (Ezek. 2:10). The entire life of Jonah was a perpetual lament. Habakkuk and Micah are woven with this same tapestry of lament. The life of Jesus, Stephen, Paul, James, Peter, and John in the New Testament also show the hope of lament.

What if we actually got together as a community and aired our complaints, not to "solve them" *per se*, nor to try and cement the grief into our hearts? What if we actually gave people space to bring their darkness to light so we could bear a burden with a brother or sister?

You see, lament has an aim. The focus is to trust God. In order to trust God, there must be an ability to take complaints to Him. O'Connor says, "Without complaint there is no lament form. Although laments appear disruptive of God's world, they are acts of fidelity. In vulnerability and honesty, they cling obstinately to God and demand for God to see, hear, and act."[2]

I remember the first time I realized a struggle with depression. I was a four-year-old sitting in our apartment in Ferguson, Missouri. No, I didn't understand the word "depression," but I keenly remember being profoundly sad and overwhelmed for what seemed to be no reason at all. As I grew up, I came to understand "the dark night of the soul," but I also did not have much language to express this, especially after I became a Christian.

Yet after I started to read through the Scriptures, especially the Psalms, I came to understand the earthiness of the language the scriptures use, and that God invites His children to this kind of dialog. I began learning how to vocalize my darkness—darkness caused by both depression and being violated in various ways. When I was able to better express my pain, I started to have an expanded view of what biblical fidelity actually looked like. There are two hallmarks of lament, in complaint that finds its trust in God. First, lament is deeply relational. Second, lament is powerfully hopeful.

Deeply Relational

Ultimately, complaint that finds its trust in God is rooted in a deep relationship. I remember a time in my early twenties when I was profoundly overwhelmed. I would tell God,

"I'm angry!" Yet this type of language simply did not convey what was going on. It was at this time I learned lament is not only a matter of vocalizing words. So, I went into the middle of the woods and said, "God, this is my prayer to You. I will not move until You speak to me." I then took a baseball bat and absolutely knocked the mess out of a tree. I hit it over and over and over until my hands would not hold the bat. I sat down in the depths of my grief and waited on God.

It was in that moment I sensed Him tell me, "Do not be afraid. You are loved. Never will I leave you or forsake you." It was as if dozens of His promises from the Scriptures were being sung over me. In this moment of utter weakness I found out God was simply asking me to be honest with Him. No gloss. No veneer. Just honesty.

As Jones says:

> The "deepest truth" about ourselves is neither that we are self-sufficient nor that we are weak, needy, and fallible; it is that we are created for communion with God, with one another, and with the whole Creation. We need God and others both to discover who and whose we are and also because it is only through our life together that we can fulfill our destiny for communion in God's Kingdom.[3]

We don't have to flatter God with platitudes to be in right relationship with Him. Over time, as we learn to grieve and lament, we can experience a deep honesty that says He is big enough not simply to receive praise, but is also strong enough to walk with humanity in pain. But in our own lives, it would often seem like our relationship with God is in crisis when bad things happen. Those who believe in God tend to have an innate sense that He is good. Yet sometimes the experiences of our lives do not match up to who we think God should be. Is this all bad? No.

The truth is, when someone has been violated, they can either say, "God, you let this happen! I do not trust in You!" and then turn their back to walk away—or they can say, "God, I feel like You let this happen! This does not match with the Bible's claim that You are a God of love and mercy! What is going on?" Then the person can choose to wrestle these thoughts out with God. From this well of honesty, a true relationship can be formed. And we have freedom to come to God with the messes of life, not just a positive attitude. As Christian Wiman says, "What is the difference between a cry of pain that is also a cry of praise and a cry of praise that is pure despair? Faith? The cry of faith, even if it is a cry against God, moves toward God, has its meaning in God, as in the cries of Job."[4]

As Ellington has said, "A relationship of trust, intimacy, and love is a necessary precondition for genuine lament."[5] When a person can vocalize the most profound depths of struggle, it not only leads to more trust, but it comes from a place of trust. Talking about the positive aspects of life is easy. There is nothing wrong with this, but when we realize the darker thoughts of life can be entrusted to One who will not only hear them, but take them seriously, it's faith-transforming. When relationship with God is taken so seriously, the deepest questions can be brought to Him (and this can be seen as an act of faith in itself!). When we're able to come to God with our pain, "from faith for faith" (Rom. 1:17) isn't dependent only on the positive parts of life, but on the totality of life. In order to understand how this is possible, it is necessary to consider the idea of "faith" in greater detail.

Biblical faith can be summed up with the words "honest togetherness." The Bible even gives a name to Jesus that encapsulates this concept—Immanuel, which means, "God with Us." Faith is not some type of "blind leap." Faith must be framed in relational terminology, since the Gospel is ultimately relational. It is the Good News about God reconciling us to Himself, ourselves, our neighbors, and the rest of creation. "Honest togetherness" comes with the idea that we can express ourselves with complete openness to God, no matter how atrocious our trials! When we wait on God with our harsh realities, we can know the walk of faith is big enough to hold the ups and downs of the relationship. Without this, the relationship mainly becomes utilitarian in nature, instead of relational.

When a relationship is deep, both praise and silence have their place. In my marriage with Amber, we neither always praise nor always complain, nor do we always talk or are we always silent. When you live in a good relationship there are diverse forms of expression while we remain present toward the other. Our relationship with God should be the same.

This is why the Biblical literature gives dozens upon dozens of cases where the way forward in relationship to God is to vocalize pain. Then we wait for God to answer, and that process may take years! Then a deeper, more true form of praise will eventually break forth. But this deeper praise doesn't come at the cost of the devastation, but is another form of redemption breaking forth.

Powerfully Hopeful

Hopeful lament is a much-needed paradoxical truth. Complaining and finding trust in God gives space to express the entire corpus of life before a God who not only hears, but is present. In Zechariah 9:11–12, the prophet tells the people they will be set free from their "waterless pits" and they should return to their stronghold, "O prisoners of hope." The brilliant paradox of being "imprisoned to hope" is a powerful word picture of the strength of imprisonment being turned on its head for good. Imprisonment is ordinarily an adverse constraint that keeps people from freedom, yet the power grace gives us imprisons us to hope precisely because God calls his people to come to him with our whole lives. When this happens, lament is hopeful instead of something that has to be avoided.

Anatomy of Lament

In order to come to a faithful, biblical understanding of complaining and finding trust in God, we will explore an anatomy of lament. Lament has three components: violation, vocalization, and victory.

Jesus uses a fictional story in Luke 18:1–8 not only to tell people how to persevere in prayer, but also how not to lose heart. In Jesus's parable, there was a widow who had experienced massive injustices. She had tasted the dregs of violation. In response, she went to the judge and vocalized the pain and wrongdoing she suffered. The unjust Judge kept ignoring her vocalizations until the widow annoyed him so much that he gave her justice and victory.

Jesus goes on to say that God is not unrighteous, but righteous. Therefore, how much more justice will He bring about for his elect? Yet Jesus asks if He will find this type of faith when he comes again. Jesus was not interested in the perseverance of perpetual prayer alone. He was asking if He would also find this type of lamenting prayer when he came back.

Would people be willing to recognize their pain, to face the violation, vocalize it, and then let Him give them victory? Would people see this is part of the essence of His nature? His righteousness is filled with lament. These two thoughts are not opposed. They complement each other. After all, righteousness does not turn a deaf ear to unrighteousness, but enters into unrighteousness and offers healing from the inside out. Let's take a closer look at each aspect of lament: violation, vocalization, and victory.

Violation

Violation can be easily overlooked. Few of us willingly want to deal with it. Facing a violation is something that is normally seen as a weakness, or something believers should be able to work through quickly in order to attain victory. Some fear looking at the reality of their own violation. Some may fear that coming to terms with how they've been violated could do damage if he/she actually took time to understand the depths of what happened. Yet this does not need to be the case in the path of Biblical faith. As Pemberton says, "Perfect faith casts out fear, but it does not exempt a person from feelings of deep sadness and their expression in tears . . . Let's not try to be less human than the Son of God."[6]

It's important for Christians to understand that when

something bad happens, the bad act never becomes good. It always remains bad. Yet the biblical hope is the pain and anger that comes from the violation doesn't need to become part of the victim's identity. Instead the way of forgiveness is given as a way to turn a wound into a scar. After all, even the risen Christ never fully forgets His own wounds. He still carries the marks of His wounds on his risen body.

Tragedy strikes. A baby dies in their parent's arms. A wife sees her husband draw his last breath. The pain of depression overwhelms you to the breaking point. An overwhelming sense of doubt can be paralyzing. A friend betrays you. These searing incidents can bring people to a breaking point. Many times the expected Christian response is to "suffer silently," or at least find a quick and easy way to become positive about the situation. But "suffering silently" isn't a badge of honor. When we've been violated, having to suck it up can strangle the life out of us.

One of the hallmarks of Western society is the desire to feel good as quickly as possible, and many times, no matter what the cost. Everyday sadness must be rejected and tragedies quickly overcome. After all, who wants to be around a person mourning death, divorce, or some other destruction for longer than a few weeks, let alone months or years!

Christians aren't immune to this. In fact, sometimes we are the worst perpetrators. But the Scriptures have a breadth beyond the Christian's need to always have "good feelings" and thoughts such as joy and happiness. The Scriptures also give voice to the darker thoughts of life, such as mourning and doubt. "Our hearts may cry out with all the anguish and rage expressed in biblical lamentation, but our contemporary liturgies provide very few ritualistic means for expressing our grief, despair, and anger in the presence of others and in the context of faith."[7]

The exploration of lament comes into even sharper focus when it collides with our faith. "The prayer of lament arises from an experience that challenges belief: a tragic event is followed by God's subsequent lack of response to prayer, thus raising questions and doubts about the nature of God's relationship with His people. Lament places a strong affirmation of belief, that God is a God who hears and delivers, over against an experience of God's silence and hiddenness in times of need."[8]

The way forward in the middle of tragedy is lament because we know we can speak honestly even when oceans of doubt attempt to cripple us. This type of honesty opens the doorway to see a God of grace. God not only sees our pain, but He feels the pain Himself. As we honestly lament, God brings healing. But it's not superficial healing only focused on how we praise God. Instead, He heals us by being present with us.

Worship focused on recognizing God's presence makes way for sufferers to realize the gateway to living: through the path of lament, forgiveness is found. So, in view of this, we'll move on and focus on the definition of lament and a couple of its features.

Again, as way of reminder, for the remainder of this book, my working definition of lament is simply this: *lament is complaint that finds its trust in God.* This understanding of lament not only holds true for humans, but also for God Himself.

Vocalization

In *Macbeth*, Shakespeare says, "Give sorrow words; the grief that does not speak knits up the o'er wrought heart and bids it break." In order to experience healing from the ways we've been violated, we must take seriously that we move to a point of vocalizing what has happened. When someone is violated, the ensuing attacks of shame will persist if voice is not given to the offense.

"Until pain is exposed and grief expressed, there can be no move toward renewal."[9] Or, as Richard K. Fenn rightly notes:

> We are on holy ground here, when untold agony begins to find its voice. If there ever is a sacred moment, it is when a soul whose torment has been suppressed and silenced finally begins to speak. Such moments occur when rituals fail, and the dead lie unburied. Such moments occur when grief, long buried below the surface of consciousness, finally breaks through, perhaps years later, and tears flow at long last. These are moments that could bind humankind into one family.[10]

My wife, Amber, has always done a masterful job of allowing me space to simply vocalize my pain. I've said dozens of times, "I don't think I need this to be fixed, but I just need to get it off my chest." This has allowed for me to not "live in my head," while also not giving me license to act like a fool. Vocalizing my pain and anger isn't really about solving a problem. It is more about knowing she is with me and prays with me. Over time, Amber's faithful presence allows me to begin seeing things differently and I know I'm not alone. I learn this also by steeping myself in the Scriptures that speak of voicing violation.

At times, the Bible can seem so foreign and irrelevant to the modern world. But hearing biblical voices of lament gives modern communities hope. We can begin to reorient our faith and see the significance and sacredness of voicing violation in our own context. As we give voice to violation within our own context, we also understand that devastation need not have the last word. Edward Hirsch says:

> We live in a superficial, media-driven culture that often seems uncomfortable with true depths of feeling. Indeed, it seems as if our culture has become increasingly intolerant of that acute sorrow, that intense mental anguish and deep remorse which may be defined as grief. We want to medicate such sorrow away. We want to divide it into recognizable stages so that grief can be labeled, tamed, and put behind us.[11]

In trying to "conquer our pain," or quickly move on from the minor keys of life to play a happier tune, we become less human. The Bible gives a different way forward. A path of honesty. A path of hope. Yet this way is going to prophetically call us back to the ways of the God of the Bible to be in the faithful presence of the One Who not only cares, but helps us bear our burdens. We don't have to simply try to get over our pain, or jump into praise, to medicate away our darkness.

Knowing we can express our pains and sorrow to a faithful God, we'll turn our attention to a specific book of the Scriptures. There we can learn to take our pains seriously and pray out our pain. When we pray our pains to God, we can know we're not ultimately defined by them, and we'll see a God who is Immanuel, God with Us.

CHAPTER 3

Lament in the Old Testament Psalms

Amber and I have been through some breathtakingly brutal times in life. We've experienced great betrayal. We've had our words misconstrued and been blamed for attacking those who we disagree with simply because we do not hold the same views. We have been accused of wrongdoing and guilt has been cast on us, even without the ability to talk through it and see if it was true.

This type of slander and malice has left us so disoriented at times that in the moment all we felt like we could do is take the next breath, put one foot in front of the other, and simply try to remain faithful. We had done everything we knew how to do. We had sought advice from mentors; we had said things that were tough, but true, and still we both felt like the insecurity of the people who had hurt us ultimately won. We believed what we had done was right, but the pain felt unbearable and we did not know how to keep going.

It was at this time I went to counseling. (I have been in and out of counseling and highly recommend it for all people when it is needed.) In this specific time of counseling I had a "lightbulb" moment. My counselor started talking with me about the liveliness and honesty of the Psalms. He had me go home with profoundly difficult questions that I unpacked with Amber, but then he gave me poignant passages from the Psalms. His purpose in having me read the Psalms wasn't to "give me answers," but simply to give me language to understand where I was, amidst my pain and disillusionment.

What I learned reading the Psalms is God's people had a prayer book that encouraged praying their pain. In reading the Psalms, I was given examples of expressing pain instead of allowing my own pain to consume me. I was able to incorporate it into my story and understand its significance, while not making the pain ultimate. In short, I was learning how to be honest, both with deep disillusionment and the risk of walking in healing. I was learning the art of lament.

There are many examples of lament in the Bible (several were given previously). Fortunately, God gave prominence to the poets who wrote the Psalms. The Psalms subversively call mankind into the exquisite nature of language. The compressed words, cadence, structure, and silence poets use in order to speak in a myriad of ways is one of the great reasons God gives such precedence to their voice in the sacred text. It is these words that provocatively called me to learn how to pray my hurt and hate, so I could learn how not to become a hateful person.

N.T. Wright says, "The Psalms represent the Bible's own spiritual root system for the great tree we call Christianity."[1] This spiritual root system is well worth exploring, especially the Lament Psalms. Oftentimes, we associate the psalms with praise. But while there are plenty of those kinds of psalms, a large portion are dedicated to lament. Pemberton notes that 40% of the entire 150 Psalms are the genre of lament. It is the largest genre in the entire book. He goes on to say the book of praise turns out to be a book of lament. If you combine this reality with the words of John Calvin, "The Psalms are an anatomy of all parts of the soul," it's critical to understand how huge a part of the soul was meant to worship.

The Psalms are not simply random songs. They are the hymnal of the Church, and we'd do well to get acquainted with them. The Psalms are broken up into five books. We will look at one psalm per book in order to get a general orientation of how lament is expressed in each.

Psalm 13

Psalm 13 is a well known Lament Psalm. It is this poem that gives an outline for understanding the anatomy of lament: violation, vocalization, and victory. The psalmist is clearly upset with his situation, and God seems to be at an incredible distance: "How long, O Lord? Will you forget me forever?" It is a prodding of God in order to see if He even cares. After all, the first four sentences start off with, "How long, O Lord?"

Yet the psalmist refuses to let a dire situation lead to silence. He wants God to answer, undoubtedly, because of the personal need to find relief, but he also takes it a step further: he asks for deliverance because his enemies would be able to claim a victory, and thus bring shame on God, since the psalmist is known to be a person of God.

The third stanza gives a picture of victory, not so much because of the praise that accompanies it (although that is part of the situation), but because, no matter what, the psalmist has been able to come to the conclusion that God has not given up on him, and therefore God has dealt bountifully with him. Notice, it does not seem as if the external situation has changed, *per se*. Instead, because the psalmist could come to God with the darkest of thoughts, and this could be counted as an expression of faith, he also had the ability to recognize the goodness of God, even though the situation had not changed yet.

In Glenn Pemberton's book, *Hurting with God*, he says,

> Psalm 13 weaves together doubt/faith, sorrow/joy, and death/life to convey not only descriptive information but also wide-ranging emotion. The poet is exhausted from pain with no energy to cope with another loss and too tired for more words. But he turns to God, placing hope in what only exists in the imagination and is only possible if God breaks through, and promising praise, confident in what God has yet to do."[2]

Psalm 43

The psalmist is profoundly disoriented with his circumstances and is dismayed that God seems to have completely left him alone. He is being oppressed by his enemy, but while he is seeking refuge in God, God seems to have rejected him. But the writer does not give up hope. Instead, the psalmist's way forward is to beg God again to "send out Your light and Your truth." In the meantime, the request does not mean waiting for God to answer—the psalmist takes on a practice that is powerfully hopeful by preaching to his own soul! It's as if the writer looks in a mirror and demands of himself to not give in to the desperation. His complaining is meant to help him find trust in God that comes from a personal demand to his own soul that the turmoil should not have the last word. Instead of falling into despair, what can he do? "Hope in God!" The last word is not the desperation and the last word is not silent resignation. The last word is a demand for hope. A demand for trust. A demand for victory.

Psalm 85

Psalm 85 takes on the definite texture of our themes violation, vocalization, and victory while it clears the path of lament. A path that ultimately leads to hope. The first stanza recalls God's redemptive history to bring restoration into the present. Just like God restored Jacob, the psalmist is asking God to do the same. N.T. Wright says, "This is what poetry and music themselves are there to do: to link the present to the past, to say, 'Remember,' to say, 'Blessed be God,' even when the tide is running strongly in the wrong direction . . . Just remember. Bring the past into the present, and that will sustain us as we wait in the dark for your future."[3]

The second stanza is a provocative statement that asks God, even in the face of communal guilt, if He will be angry forever. This is courageous language. The psalmist recognizes his own guilt and the guilt of his community. Yet he is still filled with faith, which is evidenced by his question that asks if God will be angry forever and not forgive them. The second stanza brims with honesty and the second, third, and fourth stanzas are then able to proclaim The Lord has to be near to those who fear Him. The reason the Lord must be near is because that is what the Lord promises. This is a call to the Lord to be who He said He would be. Consider the picture given in the first stanza. It references Jacob (from Gen. 32), a name which means "Deceiver." But Jacob eventually came to be known as "Israel," which means "Strives with God." Jacob was given this name because he had the courage to wrestle with God. He was finally honest enough with himself to stop practicing self-deception. He turned to God, he was tenacious, and wouldn't let go until he received a blessing.

This picture of wrestling is a powerful insight into the life of lamenting with hope. Wrestling with God is recognition that something is not right, yet it's a way to face God and say, "I am lacking. Something is wrong. Only You can make it right. I refuse to leave until you bless me. Yes, I have been wrong. I have been deceitful. Now, I want to strive with You, instead of against You." Recalling God's victorious history and bringing it into the present moment creates a new narrative of hopeful faith—a faith that has the tenacity to complain to God. But it's a complaint that finds its trust in God and refuses to let go. Even if it costs us an injury like Jacob's hip being put out of place.

Psalm 90

Psalm 90 weaves in images of creation, while acknowledging the shortness of human life compared to the eternity of God.

The image of God being the intended dwelling place shows us a picture of trust and security. This trust and security existed before mountains sprang up, and before humanity walked the earth.

Yet the psalmist goes on to say that God's anger results in people being "brought to an end." Since the iniquity of the people is in clear sight of God, it feels like all of their days are passing away under His wrath. This paints a provocative picture that confesses, "We are guilty! Will you not forgive? Will you punish us forever? We are small. We are a mist!" The presence of guilt and the need for forgiveness is real. Yet the psalmist continues to plead with God to not remain in His anger. The psalmist says the best way forward is for God to teach the people to number their days. Human life is incredibly short. But they still need to be satisfied with His love the very first thing in the morning. If this could happen, then the people would experience hope-filled lament.

Psalm 137

Psalm 137 is a picture of violent outrage, and many cringe at the imagery. Yet Brueggemann offers a different insight:

> At first glance, Psalm 137 strikes us as a childish outburst. On reflection, it may be the voice of seasoned religion which knows profoundly what it costs to beat off despair. More than simply knowing the cost, this speaker is prepared to pay! What it costs is conceding even our wish for retaliation to the sovereignty of God, who is beyond our ways of acting (Isa. 55:8, 9). It could

be that this psalm occurs in a context in which God's ways and thoughts for vengeance are "higher," but that does not keep Israel from speaking it honestly to the throne. It is an act of profound faith to entrust one's most precious hatreds to God, knowing they will be taken seriously.[4]

Bartow adds:

Could it be that hearing and speaking the biblical laments—and not editing them so as to render them less disturbing—has something to do with loving one's enemies and not hating them, however much the language of hatred may appear in the biblical laments themselves? . . . Endlessly I have heard complaints about the savagery of this lament, but seldom have I heard any outcry against the savagery—not of words, but of deeds—of Edom and Babylon. Strange that wanting too much to be nice can bring about solidarity with the tyrant and the oppressor, and condemnation of the tyrannized and the oppressed. Better, I should think, to have it the other way around: to bear with ancient Israel—and with others in our own times—in their distress, tears, and fury. Better to hear and voice the complaint of the abused, neglected, and angry than to become deaf to their cries and mute concerning their plight. Better also to brave the storm in our own inner being in the face of atrocities committed against us than to attempt to deceive God about how we actually feel . . . Honest lamentation then, however bitter, may flow from a heart set right with God

> through frank acknowledgment and confession of its condition.[5]

In view of these Lament Psalms, it is critical to see that vocalizing suffering, rejection, and pain are essential to a life of true faith. The Bible leaves no room for silent resignation in the face of atrocity. In fact, it is this type of vocal lament that helps to set the pace for the soul to understand victory. But victory is not only constrained to praise and thanksgiving, but finds a voice in the midst of doubt and pain.

Though my overview of the Psalms is by no means exhaustive, the voice of lament permeates this book, along with the rest of the Old Testament. The examples given also show the diversity of reasons for lament and tune our hearts with God's concern for justice. When the theme of forgiveness as lament appears in our biblical studies, we're reminded that it is no minor theme, but is essential to practicing a healthy Christian faith.

Over the course of serving at His Voice Global, I've been profoundly moved by observing how the South Sudanese mourn. I have attended several funerals, and they literally last for days. There is public crying, open mourning, and deep expressions of anguish. Unlike most Americans, South Sudanese understand that expressing grief over death and tragedy is not the antithesis of faith. In fact, it is an expression of faith. So, to my brothers and sisters in the West: please have ears to hear and eyes to see. Those who many consider to be "the least of these" are teaching us. In fact, as much as I've taught on this subject, I've learned much more by living alongside our African brothers and sisters.

As I mentioned at the beginning of this chapter, going

through deep pain in life and ministry is significant. It can be profoundly disorienting, whether it is a death of a person, a death of a dream, or the death of a relationship. My prayer is that you would see there is a rich biblical language in the Psalms. The Psalms are our prayer book that show us how to engage the devastations of life. May we grow to be a people who can walk honestly with the Lord and learn to steep in the Psalms amidst everyday life. The Psalms provide a language of hope in the middle of our darkness. Just like my counselor and South Sudanese brothers and sisters, may you find a faithful God in the Psalms who is ever with you, not only in the good times but also in the middle of darkness. You are His. You are loved.

CHAPTER 4

Forgiveness as Lament for Humanity

So far, we've explored the biblical basis for lament. We now turn our gaze to consider how forgiveness is one of the expressions of lament. We made the case that lament is an expression of worship. Lament is a form of forgiveness that needs to be recovered in our culture. Lament is not only a faithful form of worship, it's necessary for our spiritual wellbeing. As we learn to express our lament, it's important to see how lament and forgiveness go hand-in-hand, because forgiveness is at the foundation of Christianity. Not all lament is forgiveness, yet all forgiveness has lament as part of its DNA. In fact, the lack of learning to lament has directly led to the roots of not knowing how to forgive. Much like the previous chapters, we'll look at the anatomy of forgiveness through the same lenses of violation, vocalization, and victory.

As I began learning how to walk in forgiveness towards my mom, I felt a bit like a fumbling toddler. Yet I truly believe God stuck His hand out and taught me how to walk. Now that I am on this journey, it is still a choice every day to walk in forgiveness. This is not a burden, but simply an invitation every moment of every day to live a life of forgiveness. We all need grace as we fumble along the path of forgiveness.

Defining Forgiveness

Christian forgiveness is not seeking revenge for a wrong done. Instead, forgiveness relinquishes the desire for the offender to pay you back and seeks reconciliation and restoration with the one who caused the hurt. Notice, forgiveness is opposed to vengeance, not justice. As Lewis Smedes notes:

> Vengeance is our own pleasure of seeing someone who hurt us getting it back and then some. Justice, on the other hand, is secured when someone pays a fair penalty for wronging another even if the injured person takes no pleasure in the transaction. Vengeance is personal satisfaction. Justice is moral accounting. Forgiving surrenders the right to vengeance, it never surrenders the claim of justice.[1]

There have definitely been times in my own story I have wanted to seek vengeance—and many times I unfortunately decided this was the best route. Yet, when I pray my desire for vengeance, rather than fantasize about it, God meets me with grace to walk a different path, even when it seems like a long time before an answer comes.

Vengeance leads a violated person down an endless path of misery, but Jesus offers the path of forgiveness as a way to stop the misery. Smedes continues:

> There are only two genuine options for responding to a personal injury that we did not deserve. One of them is vengeance. The other is forgiving . . . The reason getting even does not make life fairer is that it never happens. Cannot happen. Ever. Not a chance of it. Will the Tutsis ever get even with the Hutus? Will the Bosnian Muslims ever get even with the Serbs? Will the Bloods ever get even with the Crips on the streets of Los Angeles? Never. They may go on killing each other until they are all dead, but they will never get even. The bodies broken and blood spilled in the futile fight to even the score mock the rationality of the human race.
>
> The reason we cannot get even is that the victim and the victimizer never weigh pain on the same scale. One of us is always behind in the exchange of pain. If we have to get even, we are doomed to exchange wound for wound, blood for blood, pain for pain forever. Perpetual pain. Perpetual unfairness.[2]

Jesus gives some galvanizing words in His famous Sermon on the Mount (Matt. 5–7) that inform not only the forgiveness of friends, but of those who have hurt others to the point that they have become enemies.

> You have heard that it was said, "You shall love your neighbor and hate your enemy." But I say to you, Love

> your enemies and pray for those who persecute you, so that you may be sons of your Father who is in heaven. For he makes his sun rise on the evil and on the good, and sends rain on the just and on the unjust. For if you love those who love you, what reward do you have? Do not even the tax collectors do the same? And if you greet only your brothers, what more are you doing than others? Do not even the Gentiles do the same? You therefore must be perfect, as your heavenly Father is perfect.
>
> —Matt. 5:43–48

Undoubtedly, these are some of the most difficult words in all of Scripture. Jesus says that instead of hate, we should return love. But the pattern toward loving starts with prayer. When love seems impossible, pray. It is in this act of grace that people can come to the realization they do not need to "conjure up" forgiveness. Instead, it is a grace gift that is given.

It is in prayer that one first comes to a God who feels the pain of the violation even more deeply than the one who was violated. It is in seeing a God who presently hurts over the pain of his children that one can come to understand the faithfulness of God.[3] It is in prayer one can see a picture of a God who enters into the pain of his people and offers healing from the inside out, from the violated to the violator. This is why Jesus asks those who have been violated to pray for the violator.

It is also in prayer that the violated come to hear restoration of their own humanity. In other words, those who have been violated still matter. In learning the anatomy of forgiveness, one comes to understand the violation can be brought to God, in all of its shame, anger, humility, and pain. The violated person can come to the realization that the Suffering God has not been separated from the personal pain of the violated. God also hears the words of the violated so they're able to understand their wounds are significant in His sight. But while wounds are significant, they are not ultimate.

It is the Lamenting God who has the power to fill the wounds, by grace. God shows solidarity with the wounded in His own flesh to make the violated person's wounds miraculously heal into scars. Real pain exists and must be taken seriously. Yet, this pain and hatred are not what is ultimate. Love is. As Brian Zahnd says in *Radical Forgiveness*:

> Although hatred may be very powerful, it's love that never fails, and that love is the greatest thing of all. If we hate our enemies because they first hated us, and return hate for hate because that's what hate does, we will continue to live in the ugly world of hate and its endless cycle of revenge. But when love enters the world of hate and is willing to love even its enemies, a new and real kind of change comes to the world—a change where hate does not have the last word."[4]

When a violated person can come to the Suffering God in prayer with this sort of seriousness, it is an act of faith that shows forgiveness toward a violator is only possible with the strength of God.

This act of prayer will also lead the violated to understanding that they were once the violators. The violators of God. All of us at one time violated God. We all have turned our back on Him. Yet, even while we did this, He still deeply loved us.

An important aspect of the gift of forgiveness and not taking revenge on the violator is seeing the balm of love as an antidote. This antidote was first applied to the violated one who is now coming to a Forgiving God as a "loved child of God." As Jones says:

> The invitation to God's Kingdom, the call to conversion and new life, is an invitation to discover ourselves, not as something to be "possessed" or obsessively concerned about, but as people called into communion through forgiving and reconciling love. We are called out of our obsession with ourselves by the One who invites us to friendship with God and with one another in Christian community.[5]

Jesus tells a profound story to prove this point in Matthew 18:23–35. Peter asks how many times one should forgive another. Jesus, in saying one needs to "forgive from your heart," is immediately echoing the reality that forgiveness is not just some type of verbal articulation, but is something that comes from within and is dependent on remembering.

Jesus's asking a person to come to God first is the gift of being reminded of God's personal restoration with the individual. It's this restoration that gives one the ability to carry out forgiveness, yet it is important to see that forgiveness is not just a declaration (although it can include this). It is a lifestyle.

L. Gregory Jones gives an apt summation:

> Christian forgiveness is not simply a word of acquittal; nor is it something that merely refers backward. Rather,

> Christian forgiveness—and, more specifically, forgiven-ness—is a way of life, a fidelity to a relationship of friendship, that must be learned and relearned on our journey toward holiness in God's eschatological Kingdom. It is a way of life that requires the ever-deepening and ever-widening sense of what friendship with God and God's creatures entails. It is ever-deepening and ever-widening precisely because we must continually find ways—in community with God, one another, and the whole Creation—to unmask our deceptions of ourselves, of others, and of the world through lives of forgiven-ness.[6]

Not seeking revenge for the wrong that has been done and relinquishing the desire to be paid back personally for the wrong can be painfully difficult. In fact, forgiveness itself is a form of suffering. This is part of the "fellowshipping in the sufferings of Christ" that is spoken of by Paul in Philippians 3:10, "That I may know Him and the power of His resurrection, and may share His sufferings, becoming like Him in His death." Another passage that Paul gives us is 2 Corinthians 1:5: "For as we share abundantly in Christ's sufferings, so through Christ we share abundantly in comfort too."

Notice, it is a present sharing in the sufferings of Christ. Although these sufferings take on many forms, one of the ways in which a Christian expresses suffering is through forgiveness. After all, every time those who belong to God are hurt, He hurts. He suffers. Relationship was not broken in the Trinity during the deepest time of suffering on the Cross. Accordingly, the Triune God calls his people to participate in the intra-Trinitarian relationship during their deep times of suffering.

When one shares in the sufferings of Christ through resting in the grace of the intra-Trinitarian relationship, the possibility of reunification with the offender is opened up. The Suffering God offers restoration and inside-out healing amidst the pain of the situation.

Understanding God has personally restored the one who is now the violated, the desire for restoration with the violator is now possible. This does not mean the violator will always want reunification, nor does it even mean they will recognize their violation. But it does allow the one violated to offer the gift of reconciliation, even if it is not received.

Undoubtedly, it can be an incredible struggle when the person who has hurt you will not own what they have done. I personally struggled this way for quite some time with my mom. I would hear comments like "I tried the best I could," but these comments didn't help, they were crushing. I would think to myself, "If this is the best, that is pretty messed up." Yet, over the course of time, I grew to understand (and still need to speak this to myself) that she never needed to own what she did in order for me to forgive her.

Jones continues:

> Forgiveness is not so much an action performed, or a feeling felt as it is an embodied way of life in an ever-deepening friendship with the Triune God and with others. As such, a Christian account of forgiveness ought not simply or even primarily to be focused on the absolution of guilt; rather, it ought to be focused on the reconciliation of brokenness, the restoration of

> communion—with God, with one another, and with the whole creation.[7]

Notice, Jones makes a keen observation that guilt should not be overlooked, yet guilt is not ultimate. If guilt is not recognized, by definition forgiveness is not needed. Therefore, a recognition of violation is essential to truly walking in forgiveness. Yet, if the aim is "reconciliation of brokenness," then the recognition of the violation is a means to the end of walking in forgiveness.

This matters a great deal for those who would struggle to forgive others for the wrongs committed against them. This means in part that no matter how difficult the process of forgiveness is for those who have been violated, we can forgive even when those who have harmed us are unable to acknowledge the harm in the same way you would articulate it. It also means forgiving others is a process, and you can know you are forgiven even as you struggle with anger yourself. You can know that true, deep forgiveness is not a matter of "forgive and forget." But perhaps the late Dr. Martin Luther King Jr. can give us some insight into this.

Acknowledging the Violation

One of the greatest sermons ever preached on loving enemies was given by Dr. Martin Luther King Jr. during the Civil Rights Movement in America. The main points of his sermon are so profound, I'll use them as an outline for how we might walk in forgiveness ourselves: "Forgiveness does not mean ignoring what has been done or putting a false label on an evil act. It means, rather, that the evil act no longer remains as a barrier to the relationship . . . When we forgive, we forget in the sense that the evil deed is no longer a mental block impeding the relationship."[8]

As Dr. King notes, it's impossible to forgive without first realizing something wrong has been done. This first pathway, acknowledging violation, is expressed in countless ways. When we see a wrong has occurred, violation can be taken seriously. Yet, there's another step. We must realize the wrong that has been done will never be right. Far too many times people try to convince themselves and others that somehow wrongdoing will eventually be "all right." The truth is that it will never be "all right." Remember, forgiveness predicates the reality something wrong actually needs to be forgiven. In fact, forgiveness is negated if the wrong is somehow undone.

A great deal of freedom can be experienced when we stop trying to make what is wrong turn out right. We have to remember again and again, when something bad happens, the bad act never becomes good. It always remains bad. Yet, through a biblical worldview, the pain and anger caused by a violation do not need to become part of the victim's identity. Instead, the way of forgiveness is given, so a wound can become a scar. Even the risen Christ never fully forgets His wounding. He still carries the marks of crucifixion on His risen body. But the void of the wound has been filled in with flesh to become a scar.

The capacity to wound is not coequal with the capacity to heal, because good is infinitely stronger than evil. The hope of forgiveness has the ability to take the violation seriously while making room for a victim to not ultimately be defined by their wound. The provision of forgiveness in Jesus is infinitely stronger than any devastation.

So far, I've made the case that it's essential for a victim to take their violation seriously in order to come sufficiently to terms with it. This is a precursor to vocalizing their violation. And all of this needs to happen before forgiveness can truly be extended. In fact, remembrance is part of the testimony of the sacrament, the Lord's Supper. Every time Christians come together to take the Lord's Supper, a significant part is the act of remembrance. In Matthew 26:28, it's written that Jesus emphasizes remembrance that his blood was spilled for the forgiveness of sins. It's remembrance of violation and sin, not silencing or covering up, that is key to forgiveness.

Vocalization

The importance of vocalizing violation cannot be expressed enough. Silent resignation only leads to internal chaos getting the last word in the life of the one who's been violated. When this chaos reigns, the possibility of forgiveness remains in the distant future as something that should happen but can't ever be attained.

Desmond Tutu, who has brilliantly led the way of forgiveness in South Africa, poignantly notes:

> We must each be especially courageous and name the hurts that cause us to feel shame or diminish us. When our dignity is violated, it serves no one if we stuff the injury away in the closet of our disowned past. We do not need to succumb to the temptation to meet such a violation with retaliation. The only way to heal this hurt is to give voice to what ails us. It is only in this way

> that we can keep our pain and loss from taking root inside us. It is only in this way that we have a chance for freedom.[9]

Earlier in this book, we explored the Lament Psalms in order to learn how breathing out deep complaints and hatreds goes beyond mere catharsis. The movement of these psalms is a calculated path of faith that is a way for vocalizing our pains to God. God gave us a blueprint for lament so a victim and victimizer have a chance to walk in forgiveness and live their humanity more deeply. When we fail to lament the way God intends, we will inevitably express violence to ourselves or to the violator.

Volf says:

> By placing unattended rage before God we place both our unjust enemy and our own vengeful self face to face with a God who loves and does justice. Hidden in the dark chambers of our hearts and nourished by the system of darkness, hate grows and seeks to infest everything with its hellish will to exclusion. In the light of the justice and love of God, however, hate recedes and the seed is planted for the miracle of forgiveness. Forgiveness flounders because I exclude myself from the community of sinners. But no one can be in the presence of the God of the crucified Messiah for long without overcoming this double exclusion—without transposing the enemy from the sphere of monstrous inhumanity into the sphere of shared humanity and oneself from the sphere of proud innocence into the sphere of common sinfulness.[10]

Yet, since prayer is not just a monologue, but a dialogue, the use of silence is just as much a part of lamenting prayer as vocalization. Two people talking at the same time is annoying. "The use of silence, questions, poetry, and metaphor in the prayers of lament all point to the intrusion of experiences that transcend the familiar and exhaust the speaker's established structures for coping."[11]

Silence in the Psalms doesn't signal God's abandonment or withdrawal, but is a form of His presence. God's silence is an aspect of relationship that gives audience to humans for the vocalization of lament. Unfortunately, fear of silence is often correlated with abandonment or relational distance, and has produced a culture of continual noise, and a deep distrust of the presence of God in the midst of silence.

Silence also gives space for human presence. Not every interaction has to be met with perpetual talking. When Job's friends came to be with him after his tragic losses, seven days of silence was exactly the proper response (Job 2:13). The problem came when they opened their mouths. Their need to talk may be an indication that they were too uncomfortable with God's silence. We know that later in the book of Job, God is highly offended by their big mouths and inability to keep quiet. I wonder if God was offended because they interrupted His tears and the tears of Job. Sometimes formalizing thoughts with words taints the sacredness of Divine tears cried over devastation. Reverence for silence creates space for humanity to understand that words are not the only way to communicate. Sometimes only tears and the non-verbal presence of another will do.

An instance of this silence in my own life was when my dad died. It was quite sudden and completely stunning. My friend Jarrett came over to my house during the ensuing two days and literally did not talk. He simply sat next to me. Honestly, it was his silent presence that spoke to me more than any words other people tried to use to bring comfort. Of course, people had great intentions, but Jarrett was the one who knew that words did not need to be said. Silent presence is what spoke deeply in a cataclysmic time of grief.

Beyond Silence

We've seen how silence can be a way of making space for another to enter into our pain with us. The silence creates a place for vocalization, a key aspect to walking the path of forgiveness.

As already stated, Christian forgiveness is not seeking revenge for a wrong done, but instead it's a relinquishing of desire for the offender to personally pay you back, as well as the desire to see reconciliation and restoration. This doesn't inherently mean spending time with the one who has caused a violation. But it does mean there's a desire to see the violator's relationship to God restored. And yet, when we personally struggle through forgiving others, we suddenly find so many ways of avoiding it. To love our enemies seems impossible. Forgiveness is easy to accept theoretically, but ultimately, it's far too difficult to put into practice. When we consider those who have offended us, it can feel impossible to even start down the path of forgiveness. So we attempt to bury the violation and "get over it."

Rather than start with the one who has caused the violation, our starting point on the path of forgiveness needs to start with God. The first question we can ask is, "God, how do you view this person?"

Several years ago, I was having a deeply difficult time trying to walk in forgiveness towards my mom. Now, I am not a person who has experienced many visions, even though I believe in them. Yet, on this day I was praying and the Lord allowed me to picture my mom playing in her backyard. She was about four years old and had this gorgeous white dress on. As she was playing, she had an awareness of her beauty. As she continued to play, she stepped in a puddle of mud and ruined her dress.

The more I meditated on this picture of my mom, the more I sensed God saying, "That is how she has chosen to live. She has lived like she is stained, instead of living like she is beautiful."

It was at this time a profound sense of compassion for her came over me. Did it make everything right that she did wrong? No. Yet it allowed me to see her from a different perspective.

The next question to be asked should be, "God, how do you forgive?" Being concise with these questions will help to properly orient us so we can see the provision of forgiveness as a gift. Only then can we even get a view of forgiveness, because we begin to recognize God has already provided reconciliation of our deepest betrayals. Not only that, but God says, "I feel your pain more deeply than you do. I know you and the person who hurt you deeper than either of you will know yourselves. Because I am a forgiving God, I am asking you to live in your identity as one who forgives."

As we walk the path of forgiveness, God asks us to live

within our identity of a victory He has declared into and over our lives. The life of forgiveness will be messy. But it's an illusion to think an alternative path offers an easier, cleaner, or better way.

Naming and Condemning the Offense

Not only is vocalizing the violation important, but it is critical to name and condemn the offense. When a victim of a violation remains quiet, it's often considered "taking the high road." Yet Christianity knows nothing of this. Instead, sin can be brought to light and the disunity can be overcome by reunity by saying the violator acted in a subhuman way. Seeking unity is a path that has enough tenacity to name and condemn the offense in order that reunification is a true option. To be clear, this path takes discernment, which many times requires the need to talk through this with a friend, pastor, or mentor.

Honesty is the true "high road." Honesty about the offense and honesty about the hope of forgiveness. On the need to vocalize, O'Connor says, "Acknowledging and reflecting back suffering restores the humanity of victims because it validates their perception of the way the world has fallen away from under their feet."[12]

Miroslav Volf has been an incredible voice in exploring forgiveness, along with the process it takes. As he points out, the first step is the need to name and condemn the wrong that has been done.[13] It's essential to understand that every time a violation occurs, the one violated has experienced a form of death. Humanity is not meant to live in disunity.

Christian forgiveness requires a sense of emulating the

death and resurrection of Jesus. As Jones says, "For as we participate in Christ's dying and rising, we die to our old selves and find a future not bound by the past."[14] Therefore, taking an offense seriously is essential in the lifestyle of forgiveness. The naming of the wrong is something that can be incredibly difficult, yet it is this naming that sets the pain to words so that chaos can be brought to form.

Victory

As we have seen with the anatomy of lament (violation, vocalization, victory), we are seeing the lifestyle of forgiveness has the same anatomy (violation, vocalization, and now, victory). The victory of forgiveness is not first and foremost the reconciliation of relationship with the person who has violated us, but recognizing Immanuel, "God with Us." The ultimate relationship in life has continued even in the valley of the shadow of death. When we see the inability of the violator to break our relationship with God, when we see that God never leaves or forsakes us, we're already walking the path of victory.

There is great comfort in bringing the violation to God, Who gives us the gift of a forgiving path. Even more, as we walk in forgiveness, we begin to realize, as Jones has said, that we do not have to be controlled by the person who hurt us. "Human sin is forgiven only because it is confronted and judged. But that judgment is wholly in the service of mercy, reconciliation, and new life."[15]

One way of learning how to forgive is learning how, truly, to pray the well-known part of the Lord's Prayer "Forgive us our debts, as we also have forgiven our debtors" (Matt. 6:12).

Rodney Reeves offers a great foundational footprint for giving insight into this prayer:

> Is Jesus really saying that God's forgiveness of my sins is contingent upon my forgiveness of others, as if God were dependent upon me for my salvation from sin? Once again, we need to pay attention to the plural form of the pronouns, which are evident in the prayer ("our debts") but hard to see in Jesus's warning ("your sins")—in fact, the entire prayer is a corporate prayer, utilizing plural pronouns. We tend to individualize sin, as if my sin is my problem and your sin is your problem. Therefore, Jesus should have taught us to pray, "Forgive my debts as I forgive my debtors"—which would make more sense since this is the prayer I am supposed to pray in my closet, all by myself. But Jesus would have us pray a corporate prayer even in our closet. We pray to "*our* Father" (he belongs to everyone). We pray for "*our* daily bread" (it takes a *village* to provide bread: farmers, millers, bakers). We pray, "lead *us* not into temptation" (when one suffers we all suffer). Indeed, the Lord's Prayer is as much a prayer for others as it is for me.
>
> Consider the implications, then, of the corporate reality of sin—a common conviction in Jesus' day. What the Jewish people recognized as a given we tend to ignore: sin is a debt to God and to others. To pretend like my sin affects no one else but me is the height of arrogance and foolishness. Therefore, since my sin affects other people (and their sins affect me), it would be equally arrogant and foolish to pretend as if God is the only

> one who needs to forgive me (it would be like saying I can hate my brother and still have a right relationship with God; Jesus thinks that's impossible, Matt. 5:22–26). Debts, sins, forgiveness—these are social realities that cannot be reduced to individual experience. Therefore, when I pray to God, "Forgive us *our* debts," I'm not only asking him to forgive my *debts* but also to forgive *my* debtor. And, if God has heard my prayer and forgiven both him and me, who am I to withhold forgiveness? (Later, Jesus told a parable making the same point, 18:21–35.) To go to God and ask him to "forgive our debts"—all of them, not just mine but the entire community—assumes I've already forgiven my debtors since I'm asking God to forgive them. So, the way Jesus set up the Lord's Prayer, we cannot pray the first part, "Forgive us our debts" without intending the last part, "as *we also have forgiven* our debtors." To hold a grudge against my debtor implies I didn't mean what I prayed—the duplicity of a hypocrite. And, Jesus made it plain that God doesn't listen to hypocritical prayers. He won't play the role of a "bit actor," especially when it comes to prayer and fasting."[16]

Learning to walk in the victory of forgiveness is supernatural, but it is not impossible. God reminds those who have been violated of the grace He has provided for them personally, that God truly did forgive them and therefore, has given an unlimited amount of forgiveness to the violator. When the violated person sees the Suffering God identify them as a "Forgiven Child," they can pass on the same possibility of reunification to the violator. In fact, when we pray, as Reeves says, the Lord's Prayer, it is mainly a corporate prayer of asking forgiveness for the community of humanity.

But it's easy to lose heart on the path of forgiveness, so it's critical not only to see how Jesus taught humanity to pray, but to see how He prayed for humanity. Before he died on the Cross, He prayed an exquisite prayer, known as the High Priestly Prayer, in John 17. Jesus has not simply left humanity in "a world of hurt," but had the foresight and vision to see suffering and violation will be part of the human experience. Yet He provides the way of grace in His prayers of protection and empowerment that make a lifestyle of reunification and forgiveness possible:

> When Jesus had spoken these words, he lifted up his eyes to heaven, and said, "Father, the hour has come; glorify your Son that the Son may glorify you, since you have given him authority over all flesh, to give eternal life to all whom you have given him. And this is eternal life, that they know you the only true God, and Jesus Christ whom you have sent. I glorified you on earth, having accomplished the work that you gave me to do. And now, Father, glorify me in your own presence with the glory that I had with you before the world existed."
>
> —John 17:1–5

First, Jesus says eternal life is to "know You the only true God, and Jesus Christ Whom you have sent." It was imperative that in His prayer eternal life was not equated mainly to a list of things that needed to be accomplished. Instead, it focused on the epicenter of Christianity: relationship. This is also why "God with Us" is the foundation of the victory of forgiveness, first between God and us. Then we extend forgiveness one to the other. God has placed us in relationships that must be reunified. Simply covering over offenses and then moving on won't do.

Next, notice Jesus prays in the present tense. He says, "I am praying for them." It is a picture of a Suffering God continuously calling out to the Father, Who is greatly moved when His children are hurt. Jesus goes on to ask the Father to "Keep them in Your name, which You have given Me, that they may be one, even as We are one." The vision is one of unity. The power of God to keep His children includes power to reunify when the bond of relationship is broken. It is something Jesus prays for right now. Presently.

He also prays, "I do not ask that you take them out of the world, but that you keep them from the evil one." He is expressing another way of saying the Lord's Prayer, "lead them not into temptation, but deliver them from evil." The disunifying and destructive way of the evil one is wrought with brokenness and unforgiveness. Yet, part of staying in the world is refusing to walk in the schemes of the evil one and live unified in the Triune God, learning to bless and pray for enemies and offer forgiveness.

Finally, Jesus prays, "As you sent Me into the world, so I have sent them into the world." As has already been stated, the essence of the Kingdom is mercy. It is entering into the pain of the world and offering healing from the inside out, a holistic healing that does not just concentrate on outward actions, but heals so deeply in the unseen places of our heart that outward actions of grace overflow.

In its essence, this is incarnational living. It is exactly how Jesus prays for His people to live. The community of

Christians is not to be insulated from suffering, pain, and rejection. Yet, they are also not meant simply to become "suffering-centric." Instead, the aim of incarnational living is to provide healing to others. Christians are meant to be agents of reunification, first with God, then self, others, and the rest of creation. They are meant to bring an anthem of honest hope, which has enough strength and faithfulness to see that the way of living into reunification comes from learning not to take revenge on someone when they are violated. Instead, we offer restoration and the grace of living a life of love to those who have sinned against us. This is what Jesus came to do. This is what the life of the Christian should express. After all, this is what Jesus is currently praying for.

Offering Restoration

All of life in Christ is found in grace. Therefore, the path of forgiveness is also a gift of grace. It is not something that needs to be conjured up in order to forgive the offender. Instead, the way is a path between the offender, the offended, and God.[17] This type of triangular understanding in forgiveness is also a death knell for one of the pitfalls Jones points out. "Those who embody forgiveness discover that one of the chief obstacles to overcome is the tendency to see one's own life as something to be either possessed or simply given over to another's possession; too often the result is that people cling to their power or even their powerlessness."[18]

Once we go back to the time in which God offered us ultimate restoration with Him in salvation, we can also see He provided the grace to forgive others when they violate us. By seeing the violator not only offend us, but also God, we have the strength to not only take our pain to God, we also can ask the Suffering God to provide us the gift of forgiveness to the one who hurt us. After all, when we hurt God through disobedience, He provides the gift of forgiveness to us, so he also guarantees to provide the gift of forgiveness for us to pass on to the person who hurt us.

Again, Dr. Martin Luther King Jr. helps us better understand the possibility of forgiveness and reunification:

> We must recognize that the evil deed of the enemy-neighbor, the thing that hurts, never quite expresses all that he is. An element of goodness may be found even in our worst enemy. Each of us is something of a schizophrenic personality, tragically divided against ourselves. A persistent civil war rages within all of our lives . . . This simply means that there is some good in the worst of us and some evil in the best of us.[19]

Knowing that each person has at least some form of goodness can help the violated one to see that if the violator chooses to walk in reunification, they are actually returning to who they were called to be, to bear the image of a loving God.

When I started to learn how to walk in forgiveness with my mom, I started to realize this lifestyle was much more like a dance than a computer program. At various unexpected times, it required me to still envision my mom as that little girl playing in the backyard with the gorgeous white dress.

As we learn that forgiveness has nothing to do with "forgive and forget," we should never think the reprehensible words "If you have truly forgiven you will not talk about it" are ever part of the lifestyle of forgiveness. May the path of being open and honest with our violations give us the ability not to be defined by wounds, and empower us to have the courage to understand our scars have a sacred story that allows us to walk in honesty.

In order to walk in this type of honesty, both in the recognition of violations and the supernatural potency of forgiveness, let's now turn the ways in which God forgives by lamenting. It is in this reality we can find space to see violations are taken seriously, yet the path forward is the paradox that the tears of God are the strength of history.

CHAPTER 5

A God Who Forgives by Lamenting

One of the greatest fears many of us hold is the fear of being abandoned. Now, when I say "abandoned," it is not just the idea of "being left alone." Some of us would love the opportunity to be "left alone" on occasion. But abandonment is different.

True abandonment comes along with the harsh notion that "you are not enough." Many people experience this "you are not enough," as the root cause of many, if not all, fears.

Two of my great friends, Steve and Meg Knox, came to serve alongside of us in northern California for a time period at an incredible place, Scott River Lodge. Steve has been a great voice of clarity and encouragement in some of my most difficult days and Meg is the one who spoke one of the deepest truths into my life.

As Amber, Steve, Meg, and I were talking one time,

I asked Steve, "Hey, do you have any insight for me?" Before Steve could say one word, Meg sweetly spoke up and said, "Vernon, I do." As she tried to talk, tears came into her eyes. In a merciful and compassionate tone, she brought me a deep sense of hope: "Vernon, I just wish you knew you were enough."

She hugged me and walked away.

You see, for so long I'd believed I wasn't enough. I don't mean a "pull yourself up by your bootstraps" type of "I am enough." I mean the way that the Father looks at all of His children and says, "I am well pleased." The Father says, "You are enough because I really do love you and have given you great ability to rest in My grace." Sadly, we all are prone to struggle with the idea that we are not enough. To this day, I struggle with this, and maybe you do, too. For some of us, that lack of "enough-ness" has lingered because we thought The Father believed we weren't sufficient. Sometimes I wonder if our belief that we are not enough is informed by our view of Who God is and especially Who He was during the time of greatest agony for Jesus, the Cross. Some of us have been taught that at the most desperate time in the life of Jesus, The Father said, "I must turn my back on You. You are not enough."

Sadly, there is a theological point of view that says the Father abandoned Jesus on the Cross. This group of people may say, "I am not saying the Father ever thought Jesus was 'not enough.'" Yet, this is exactly what that idea would ultimately lead to if The Father actually abandoned Jesus on the Cross. Again, if the ultimate essence of life is found in relationship and the greatest relationship ever known is with God in the Trinity, then if the Father would "turn His back" during the cross, it would be saying, "Jesus you are not enough for this relationship. You bearing the weight of this sin has broken my 'with-ness' with you."

But I'd like to challenge that view. If it's true that God would abandon Jesus, why would He not abandon us? If God did abandon Jesus on the Cross, doesn't that mean the Trinity was somehow "broken"? If the Father actually did abandon Jesus in the midst of sin, death, and hell roaring at him, that would mean sin has the power to break the deepest communion ever known—the communion which says, "never will I leave you or forsake you." But this unbroken communion has always said, and continually says, "YOU ARE ENOUGH!" Jesus heard this from the Father and we are also empowered with the same reality. Again, this is not an "You are enough" apart from grace. It is an infused anthem that is rooted in grace.

To stare stark abandonment in the face amidst our suffering can feel utterly hopeless. I think there is a better way of understanding the Cross and I believe we can find hope when we feel abandoned.

The Cross of Jesus Christ was a horrific act of betrayal. But again, I ask, did the members of the Trinity somehow separate from each other in that moment? According to scripture, Father, Son, and Holy Spirit were fully present. The Cross was not a place of divine abandonment, but a symphonic, triune lament. Another way to put it is that the Cross is a lament worship service. The communal lament of Father, Son, and Holy Spirit in the face of complete rejection by mankind. This lament sets the foundation for forgiveness as a type of lament and opens the path of hope after violation. My conviction is that divine abandonment is not a viable scriptural option.

In addition, we'll discover that the solidarity of lament is foundational to understanding forgiveness. First with God in Himself and then with humanity.

Divine Abandonment

Challenging the belief of Jesus's abandonment at the cross is key to understanding forgiveness as lament. As William Stacy Johnson says:

> The defining premise of the gospel is God did not abandon Jesus when he cried out. Rather, the God who is for us and with us in Jesus Christ refused to abandon Jesus in his affliction and instead raised him up. It is precisely because God was united with Jesus in his agony and refused to abandon him that we can be assured of God's refusal to abandon us.[1]

In his book *Forsaken*, Thomas McCall says:

> "We should not understand it to mean any abandonment of the humanity that Christ came to take on Himself to save. And we should not understand it to mean that the communion between the Father and the Son was disrupted or that the Trinity was in any way 'broken.' We should, however, take the cry of dereliction as a powerful expression of the identification of the Son of God with us and our predicament. And we should understand it to mean that what the Father abandoned the Son to was death at the hands of sinful people. So while the abandonment is real, it in no way implies a

> loss of contact or relationship between Father and the Son."[2]

When Jesus screamed in agony, "My God, My God, why have you forsaken Me?" on the cross, the power of Satan did not have the ability to break the intra-Trinitarian relationship. When Jesus was on the Cross, the Holy Spirit didn't stop indwelling Jesus. The Holy Spirit was fully present at the Cross, and the Spirit is the One Who empowered Jesus to cry out and ask God, "Why have You forsaken Me?". Yet these words were not met by a cold Father who turned His back on Jesus at His most vulnerable time.

First of all, Jesus laments that it *feels* as though He is being forsaken by the Father. We know this because later, Jesus cries out "Into Your hands I commit My spirit" (Luke 23:46) after the lament of God "forsaking Him." Both of these statements are a way that Jesus recognized the solidarity of the lament genre of the Psalms. "My God, My God, why have You forsaken Me?" is from Psalm 22, while "Into Your hands I commit My spirit" comes from Psalm 31. Jesus is also letting humanity know that when the depth of His forsakenness was felt, the answer of the Father was, "I have not forsaken you." This is why Jesus "commits His spirit to Him." Jesus was able to do this because the Father remained present. We too have permission to speak this way to the Father when we feel like we are drinking the dregs of darkness.

Next, to think the Father stands off and "pours wrath out on Jesus" is an untenable picture in the scripture. Undoubtedly, wrath is a biblical theme, but as McCall notes, it is not that one person in the Trinity has wrath, while another has love:

> Some "part" or "parts" of God are not against me while another part is for me. The Son does not love me and bless me while the Father hates me and curses me. Rather, it is God who is for us. No "part" or aspect of God—surely no divine person—wants to see me damned while another wants to see me saved. Not at all! God—the triune God whose essence is love—is for us . . . It matters that the incarnate Son was abandoned by God to this death, for in doing so he identifies with us and stands in for us. And it matters—indeed, it makes all the difference in the world—that the relationship of purest holy love between the Father and Son was not broken on The Cross."[3]

Finally, at the time of the crucifixion, the temple curtain was torn in two, top-to-bottom (Matt. 27:51). This shows in another way that the Trinity wasn't divided. The symbolism of this event shows the vulnerability of the Father.

> God responds to Jesus' own naked cry of lament from the cross . . . by God's own reciprocal stripping down. The rending of the curtain to the Holy of Holies signifies the exposure of the very Self of God. In a moment of excruciating sorrow, God the Father lays bare the divine Self, becoming in turn as vulnerable as the crucified Son. Blount and Charles point out that the verb *schizo* used to describe the rending of the temple curtain is the same one used in Mark's depiction of Jesus' baptism (Mark 1:10). As Jesus descended, here too fully naked, into the waters of death, the heavens were torn apart (*schizomenous*), and God was revealed. This, though,

> was a blessed event—"You are my Son, the Beloved; with you I am well pleased" (Mark 1:11)—while the second was a cursed event, a day of absolute horror. In the former, God's voice came, as it were, out of nowhere—a disembodied voice. In the latter, God split the curtain to become fully visible, as if to say, *You have longed to see me. You have used all your human cunning to lure me into the open. It was not even enough that I sent my Son, my beloved. So take a good look. Here I am!*[4]

The vulnerability of the Father, Son, and Holy Spirit is foundational to understanding the Kingdom of mercy. Rather than the Cross being the abandonment of Jesus, there was solidarity of lament within the Trinity. In other words, the Trinity complains and finds trust in Themselves (lament). Father, Son, and Holy Spirit simultaneously enter into their pain and offer the healing of their presence to Each Other as the way forward (Remember! Mercy is entering into pain and offering healing from the inside out). In fact, the curtain being torn reveals what was always present, the mercy seat!

Moltmann goes on to summarize the importance of seeing a Suffering God who loves:

> It can be summed up by saying that suffering is overcome by suffering and wounds are healed by wounds. For the suffering in suffering is the lack of love, and the wounds of wounds are the abandonment, and the powerlessness in pain is unbelief. And therefore the suffering of abandonment is overcome by the suffering of love, which is not afraid of what is sick and ugly but accepts it and takes it to itself in order to heal it . . . Through

> his death he brings eternal life to those who are dying. And therefore the tempted, rejected, suffering and dying Christ came to be the centre of the religion of the oppressed and the piety of the lost."[5]

Moltmann also considers Dietrich Bonhoeffer's contribution to this understanding of God:

> God lets himself be pushed out of the world on to the cross. He is weak and powerless in the world, and that is precisely the way, the only way, in which he is with us and helps us. Matthew 8:17 makes it quite clear that Christ helps us, not by virtue of his omnipotence, but by virtue of his weakness and suffering . . . Only the suffering God can help . . . That is a reversal of what the religious man expects from God. Man is summoned to share in God's sufferings at the hands of a godless world.[6]

God is with us even in the darkest times of life. He feels our pain more deeply than we do. When we begin to understand this, we learn to walk in a humble boldness that The Powerful King Is Our Merciful Dad and that true love is summed up by "God is love" (1 John 4:8).

The Solidarity of Lament

Even before the Cross, Jesus gives insight into the communal presence of the Trinity during times of lament caused by persecution and trial. So far, we've discussed Jesus's words from the Cross and how these sayings disprove divine abandonment. We now consider forgiveness and the cross because the solidarity of lament in the Trinity is foundational to seeing forgiveness as lament. Lament is inextricably tied to forgiveness, and when we are able to see forgiveness in that light, we're better able to understand that forgiveness is less an "event" and more of a lifestyle.

During our times of greatest difficulty, God does not flee from us; instead He is Immanuel, God with Us. Accordingly, the Father and Spirit do not abandon Jesus, either. The lamenting words of the Spirit-filled, Father-focused Jesus on the Cross in the midst of persecution give us a way forward.

In this solidarity of lament and fellowship of tears, humanity has the opportunity, through grace, to recognize the need for forgiveness and to turn to God in repentance. The Trinity was not broken by the power of sin. Rather, the Trinity remains in perfect unity of symphonic lament and offers reunification through the cleansing power and solidarity of tears. It is the tears of the Trinity that overcame death, hell, and the grave. This is the greatest paradox of history and also our deepest hope to come to a merciful God in our deepest need. The tears of God are the strength of history.

When Jesus said, "Father, forgive them, for they know not what they do" (Luke 23:34), it was a cry of lamenting forgiveness and grace that reverberated through all of history. Jesus cries out to the Father to forgive those who put Him on the Cross the day of his crucifixion. But that's not all. He asks God to forgive all of humanity. Through this Spirit-filled, Father-focused lament of tears, Jesus offers the possibility of reunification. Not once does Jesus soften the offense of the Cross. He says the violation is real and tragic. Eternally tragic. Yet, He vocalizes the pain of the violation by saying,

"They know not what they do." In this, Jesus isn't saying humanity made a mistake. No, the point is that humanity is so broken and disunified[7] that no one can fully comprehend its effects. The choice to hide (i.e., the true foundation of sin) has wrought utter violence in every sphere of society, and Jesus's tear-soaked complaint to the Father is a plea to extend forgiveness to mankind.

Again, another fount of Spirit-filled, Father-focused lament that shows solidarity in the Trinity as a foundation of forgiveness comes from Mark 15:34: "And at the ninth hour Jesus cried with a loud voice, 'Eloi, Eloi, lama sabachthani?' which means, 'My God, my God, why have you forsaken me?'" As Moltmann has poignantly noted, "Every theology which claims to be Christian must come to terms with Jesus's cry on the cross. Basically, every Christian theology is consciously or unconsciously answering the question, 'Why hast thou forsaken me?'"[8]

As we've previously discussed, this fulcrum point of history isn't where the Father abandoned Jesus. Instead, the Father drew close and stayed in unified communion with the Spirit-filled Son. Together they withstood all of the disunified chaos of sin, and this is foundational to reunifying humanity and creation in the restoration of all things. This vulnerable Father-focused cry gives us an insight into the merciful essence of the Kingdom as a path to forgiveness. The cries of Jesus show vulnerability as strength in relationship. It is a paradox.

Throughout this book, we've explored how the essence of all life is relationship as it's reflected in the intra-Trinitarian relationship—a relationship that was never broken at the Cross. The vulnerability expressed at the cross shows a counterintuitive truth: there is power in mercy. The power of mercy allows weakness. The solidarity of lament is the foundation of reconciliation and is found in the subversiveness of tears. As Brueggemann says, "We do know from our own pain and hurt and loneliness that tears break barriers like no harshness or anger."[9]

We may be uncomfortable with the idea that the vulnerability of God is a sign of true strength. But this is just another way of saying God is compassionate because the Trinity is willing to enter into suffering with us. Or, as Wiman says, "Herein lies the great difference between divine weakness and human weakness, the wounds of Christ and the wounds of man. Two human weaknesses only intensify each other. But human weakness plus Christ's weakness equals supernatural strength."[10]

I want to build out a little more on a previous idea that we just touched on. It is another lament from the Cross, found in Luke 23:46: "Then Jesus, calling out with a loud voice, said, 'Father, into your hands I commit my spirit!' And having said this He breathed His last." These final words of Jesus come from a Lament Psalm, Psalm 31. Yet again, the laments of the Old Testament are woven into the New Testament and help give foundational words to lament and forgiveness as worship. After Jesus lamented, "Why have You forsaken Me?" the Father's answer was, "I have not." If The Father had turned His back and fled from Jesus while He drew His last breath, He would have never said to the Father, "Into Your hands I commit My spirit!" The Father would not have been present to receive Jesus's spirit. The One who heard Jesus ask for forgiveness of those who knew not what they were doing was the One who did not forsake His Son at His deepest time of need. He was the same God who tenderly received the spirit of Jesus, the Faithful Forgiving Lamenter, who also gives strength and grace to humanity to receive forgiveness and to offer it to others.

The symphonic Triune lament of the Cross is foundational to forgiveness and humanity also finds solidarity in the intra-Trinitarian lament relationship. As Wolterstorff says:

> God is love. That is why he suffers. To love our suffering sinful world is to suffer. God so suffered for the world that he gave up his only Son to suffering. The one who does not see God's suffering does not see his love. God is suffering love. So suffering is down at the center of things, deep down where the meaning is. Suffering is the meaning of the world. For Love is the meaning. And Love suffers. The tears of God are the meaning of history.[11]

When we understand the depth of the Trinity's mercy, the words of McCall come crashing into the soul of humanity. "The death of Jesus does not make it possible for God to love us. The death of Jesus makes it possible for us truly to know God's love, makes it possible for us to love God."[12] God has perpetually loved humanity and the world. That means He has loved you, and me. He has never given up hope, which is why He also gives the voice of lament as the foundation for understanding the gift of forgiveness. Forgiveness not only between humanity and Himself, but also for humans to offer this same gift to each other.

If you are suffering, know that God has not forsaken you. God never forsook Jesus, and He will never forsake you. In our humanity and inability to comprehend the mind of God, it is not often clear why He allows suffering into our lives. Though this book is not about trying to crack the code of that mystery, we can know that God will never, ever forsake us in our suffering. He has not only said, "Never will I leave you or forsake you," but He also tenderly and gracefully says, "You are enough."

CHAPTER 6

Lament in the New Testament

Several years ago, I met a brilliant young boy in South Sudan through a series of profoundly unfortunate circumstances. My friend, Daniel, was six years old at the time and was going out to get firewood with his mom and little sister. As they were leaving home, Daniel's mom strapped his baby sister onto her back and they went into the forest. As they walked along, Daniel's mom unknowingly stepped on a landmine. She was killed instantaneously. Daniel had one of his legs severed, but his baby sister was completely unharmed.

As Daniel screamed out for help, he also unwrapped his sister from his dead mother's back and started to drag himself and his sister to safety.

Since that tragic event, Daniel came under the care of one of the homes His Voice Global helped to start with our partner, Bishop Elias Taban, who is the head of the Evangelical Presbyterian Church of South Sudan.

Sadly, devastating stories like these are common in South Sudan, Kenya, and India. In the past, when I became aware of stories like these, I'd store up the pain and grief so I was able to continue in my work. Don't get me wrong, I was not callous with my friends like Daniel. I wept with them. Sat with them and helped as best I could. But I still struggle to find the language of lament and often don't know how to walk with great people like Daniel.

In this chapter, we will explore how Jesus and Paul give us a path for complaining and find our trust in God. My prayer is that as we explore different facets of the New Testament you will be freed from thinking the common Romans 8:28 adage "All things work together for the good" is a phrase that should be somehow used as a "cover up" to honest grief.

My prayer is that you will also see when various tragedies strike, we can be honest with God in our pain. In our honesty, we can also learn how to walk in the freedom of forgiveness when others have harmed us.

New Testament

The New Testament is considered to be much more scarce in its voicing of lament. As far as quantity, this is true. Yet the impact of New Testament lament is strong. We will focus on the voices of lament in Jesus and Paul and see how lament is the foundation of forgiveness. Jesus, the friend of sinners, and the One Who suffers with those who suffer, gives us a prototype of hope in the middle of devastation.

Jesus as the Faithful Lamenter

In "Heaven's Prisoners: The Lament as Christian Prayer", Patrick D. Miller brilliantly articulates the life of Jesus as full of lament:

> To understand the incarnation and death of Jesus through the prism of the lament psalms is to know that both the incarnation and Jesus' death are his identification with all those innocent/righteous/faithful sufferers who have experienced the pain of human existence, the terrible absence and silence of God, and human torment, oppression, mockery, and reproach. In Jesus's death, the crucified God takes up all that suffering and becomes one with it. It is now in the very heart and being of God. The death of Jesus is the confirmation of the claim of Scripture that God knows our suffering. God knows it as one who has experienced it and as one whose child has gone through it . . . This is what we mean by a theology of the cross.
>
> But the lament opens to us not only the meaning of the person of Christ. The lament is also critical for understanding the work of God in Jesus Christ, for it is our chief clue that Christ died not simply as one of us but also as one for us, both with us and on our behalf. As we hear our human voice of lament on the lips of the dying Jesus, it now becomes crystal clear: Jesus died for our suffering as much as for our sins . . . But the reading of the death of Jesus in relation to the prayers of lament tells us that the power of the resurrection is

> not over sin alone but also over death and all its many manifestations within human life. To recover the place of lament is finally not simply a matter of our own prayers but of learning at the deepest level the meaning of God's vindication of the suffering of Christ in the resurrection. It is as much our hope in the face of pain as it is in the face of sin."[1]

Jesus not only lamented on the Cross, He was also known as a Man Who regularly expressed lament to the Father. The author of Hebrews expresses the life of Jesus in the following way: "In the days of His flesh, Jesus offered up prayers and supplications, with loud cries and tears, to Him Who was able to save Him from death, and He was heard because of His reverence" (Heb. 5:7). Notice, the loud cries and tears were a form of reverence, not anti-faith. Jesus's cries expressed a firm belief in the existence of the Father while acknowledging something was wrong. But notice Jesus wasn't silently resigned, and He didn't offer up what we normally think of as "praise." Jesus's aim was to engage a Father Who listens and is engaged by the cries of His children.

Coming before the crucifixion, the Garden of Gethsemane sets a picture of lament that is instructive in seeing the essential nature of lament in spiritual formation. Nancy Guthrie, in her beautiful book *Hearing Jesus Speak into Our Sorrow*, says, "When we listen closely to the words Jesus uttered in agony in the garden, we discover that it is not only the pain of our sorrow Jesus can relate to. He also understands the loneliness of it."[2] As Jesus goes to The Garden with his disciples in order to pray, Matthew records the events:

> Then he said to them, "My soul is very sorrowful, even to death; remain here, and watch with me." And going a little farther he fell on his face and prayed, saying, "My Father, if it be possible, let this cup pass from me; nevertheless, not as I will, but as you will." And he came to the disciples and found them sleeping. And he said to Peter, "So, could you not watch with me one hour? Watch and pray that you may not enter into temptation. The spirit indeed is willing, but the flesh is weak." Again, for the second time, he went away and prayed, "My Father, if this cannot pass unless I drink it, your will be done."
>
> —Matt. 26:38–42

First, Jesus's going into this garden is not a random event. It is a picture of "the redemption of Eden." Just as Adam and Eve were called to live in communion with God in the garden, so now, Jesus comes to live in communion with the Father. Adam and Eve were tempted and chose to sin, but Jesus withstands the temptation in the garden because of His unceasing faithfulness in adhering to the Father's will.

Next, Jesus did not keep his lament to Himself and the Father alone. He tells the disciples that He is sorrowful to the point of death. In his time of deep angst, He asks them to pray. The violation of suffering and the temptation to give up come crashing like waves on Jesus. He responds to this pressure by vocalizing His pain to the community. Silence is not an option. What threatened to be an isolating instance is brought out into the open so that community can be strengthened.

Third, Jesus openly addresses the Father with a request to

"let this cup pass." Mark gives an even more intimate account: "Abba, Father, all things are possible for you. Remove this cup from me. Yet not what I will, but what you will" (Mark 14:36). It is a divine disagreement. Jesus does not want to do something that is set before Him, and He isn't resigned to silence. Instead, He engages the Father and calls on Him to "let the cup pass." Jesus Himself shows us that it's not inherently sinful to disagree with God. Rather, it's sinful to not take our complaint to God, knowing that His will is not always our own—"Nevertheless, not as I will, but as You will." Luke 22:43 records that after Jesus prayed this way, an angel appeared to Him in order to strengthen Him. Notice, Jesus was strengthened in the middle of His weakness. Yet, without the honesty of lament, faith is broken and the relationship is disunified.

After Jesus laments before the Father the first time, He goes back to the disciples. This shows He has not given up on the community. Yet, much like our own time and place, the community is asleep. Jesus gives His community a prodding by saying, "Watch and pray that you may not enter into temptation. The spirit indeed is willing, but the flesh is weak." Not only do we pray for ourselves, we pray for those in need. When we don't pray for others, temptation can get the best of us. According to Jesus, the choice of the community to avoid the sorrows of others is sinful. When we avoid entering into the pain of others, the flesh prevails.

Finally, after Jesus speaks with the disciples, He returns again to the Father—but He isn't excited about what lays ahead. Jesus doesn't start with thanksgiving. He simply says, "My Father, if this cannot pass unless I drink it, your will be done." Notice, through this entire dialogue, Jesus has an immense personal relationship with the Father. He does not address Him as "Father," but "My Father." Yet, even in entrusting himself to the Father's ways in His suffering, Jesus shows that faithful lament does not always lead to praise. The aim of faithful lament is to make sure the relationship with God continues.

Because Jesus Himself lived a life of lament, He is also able to walk with Christians in the middle of their devastations. Guthrie says, "Jesus is inclined to speak to us in our sorrow. He's not intimidated by awkwardness or hard questions. He is drawn to brokenhearted people. He knows we're not interested in pat answers or going through the motions of politeness, sentimentality, or religiosity."[3] Jesus asked the Father hard questions, awkwardly complained to the One Who would never leave Him, and in the end, entrusted Himself to the Healer of broken hearts.

It is this exact rawness and awkwardness that has empowered me to simply be honest with God in the middle of dark times. Instead of trying to "image manage" (even in my private prayer!), I can instead lay the darkness before God and simply say, "Papa, this is what seems to be going on. Please sort it out for me. Please give me insight that is from You."

Lament in the Life of Paul

Next, we will explore Paul's letters for the theme of lament, specifically his words to the Corinthians and in Romans 8. This foundation informs how forgiveness itself is later found to be a lament. It is interesting to see that Paul (Saul) himself was present and affirming during the stoning of Stephen

(Acts 7:58). It was this instance of Stephen's faithful witness that undoubtedly informed much of how Paul saw the path of lament.

The Corinthians

When Paul writes to the church in Corinth, he displays confidence in his calling as an apostle. He laments the difficulties he faced, while acknowledging his difficulties proved he was walking in obedience:

> Already you have all you want! Already you have become rich! Without us you have become kings! And would that you did reign, so that we might share the rule with you! For I think that God has exhibited us apostles as last of all, like men sentenced to death, because we have become a spectacle to the world, to angels, and to men. We are fools for Christ's sake, but you are wise in Christ. We are weak, but you are strong. You are held in honor, but we in disrepute. To the present hour we hunger and thirst, we are poorly dressed and buffeted and homeless, and we labor, working with our own hands. When reviled, we bless; when persecuted, we endure; when slandered, we entreat. We have become, and are still the scum of the world, the refuse of all things.
>
> —1 Cor. 4:8–13

What Paul shows is what looks like failure on the surface is in fact a picture of faithfulness. He is weak, held in disrepute, hungry, thirsty, homeless, reviled, persecuted, and slandered.

Though riches look like "success" to the Corinthians, if they put their trust in them, Paul says they will be their undoing. Instead, Paul points the Corinthians to the Triune God who is faithful and present to His people in the midst of adversity. Theoretically, most Christians agree with Paul when it comes to his idea of "success." But when most people see a disheveled person sitting on a sidewalk, holding a cardboard sign, they look away. Or, when someone has experienced trial after trial in their life, many of us tend to think the suffering person brought the trouble on themselves.

In 2 Corinthians, Paul wants them to know that God is not far off from those who are afflicted. Paul writes:

> Blessed be the God and Father of our Lord Jesus Christ, the Father of mercies and God of all comfort, who comforts us in all of our affliction, so that we may be able to comfort those who are in any affliction, with the comfort with which we ourselves are comforted by God. For as we share abundantly in Christ's sufferings, so through Christ we share abundantly in comfort too.
>
> —2 Cor. 1:3–5

First, Paul addresses God as "the Father of mercies and God of all comfort". He is a God Who enters into the pain of His children. God doesn't look down us in shame when we suffer, He offers healing. This healing is so powerful that when the afflicted are comforted by God, they are emboldened to "comfort those who are in any affliction."

Personally, to know the presence of Jesus during my own difficulties has allowed me to cultivate a deep empathy for others who struggle. I'm drawn to the skeptic and disenfranchised because I too know what it feels like to feel far from God.

Another profound picture of hope comes from Paul's "jars of clay":

> But we have this treasure in jars of clay, to show that the surpassing power belongs to God and not to us. We are afflicted in every way, but not crushed; perplexed, but not driven to despair; persecuted, but not destroyed; always carrying in the body the death of Jesus, so that the life of Jesus may also be manifested in our bodies. For we who live are always being given over to death for Jesus's sake, so that the life of Jesus also may be manifested in our mortal flesh.
>
> —2 Cor. 4:7–11

Humanity is not left to prove strength or resolve in the weakness and difficulties of life. Instead, God meets us in the solidarity of lament.

A final example presented to the church in Corinth is found in 2 Corinthians 12. Paul is referring to what he calls "a thorn in the flesh." It is some type of ailment that causes him quite a bit of distress. He says,

> Three times I pleaded with the Lord about this, that it should leave me. But He said to me, "My grace is sufficient for you, for my power is made perfect in weakness." Therefore, I will boast all the more gladly of my weaknesses, so that the power of Christ may rest upon me. For the sake of Christ, then, I am content

> with weaknesses, insults, hardships, persecutions, and calamities. For when I am weak, then I am strong.
>
> —2 Cor.12:8–10

Many of us have these thorns in the flesh. It may be chronic illness, a psychological trauma, or sexual brokenness. Though we would never wish these things on anyone and we wish we could get rid of them ourselves and live trouble-free lives, God can even use these things to draw us near in dependence on Him. Though being more aware of dependence on God doesn't take away our difficulties, we can know that God walks with us through our trials.

Thankfully, Paul did not shy away from hard dialogue with God. He pleaded. He complained. Yet, like the psalmist, he ultimately found his trust in God in lament. When the Corinthian church experiences difficulty, Paul shows the faithful an example of vocalizing their lament. When lament becomes an act of spiritual formation, like Paul, we too may hear, "My grace is sufficient." Our pleading with God becomes the pathway for grace where we are finally able to say, as Paul did, "When I am weak, then I am strong."

Romans 8

Romans 8 shows us that as we lament, God's goodness derives from His presence. When we are aware that God is present, the goodness, pain, and doubt in the life of the believer have space to mingle together.

One of the main points Paul is trying to show the church at Rome is the idea that a conquering empire is not the way of the Kingdom of God. Instead, Jesus bases the foundation of the Kingdom in mercy. Therefore, it is essential to see the connection between mercy, lament, and forgiveness.

Again, the word-picture of mercy in the Bible is to enter into the pain and offer healing from the inside out. The incarnation is a great picture of this. Jesus left the perfection of Heaven and came into the world, not in to condemn it, but to offer hope and healing. As it says in John 3:16–17, "For God so loved the world, that he gave his only Son, that whoever believes in him should not perish but have eternal life. For God did not send his Son into the world to condemn the world, but in order that the world might be saved through him." Jesus came to restore relationship between God, man, and the rest of creation. Yet, He did not do this by the demanding ways of Caesar. He came to seek and save that which was lost (Matt. 18:11). Jesus came to serve, not be served (Mark 10:45). Jesus came in the way of mercy.

In this view of the theme of mercy, Romans 8 is a lament wrought with hope. First, Paul points out that creation groans (v. 22), humans groan (v. 23), and the Holy Spirit groans (v. 26). One of the reasons all three are groaning is because of the recognition that something is wrong. Yet the belief that something is wrong comes from a deep-seated belief that something should also be right. These groans have hope and it is hope in a God Who hears and enters into the pain of His people and the world.

Next, though Paul knows he's not condemned, he quotes a Lament Psalm, Psalm 44: "For your sake we are being killed all the day long; we are regarded as sheep to be slaughtered." As has been discussed earlier, the Psalms offer a spiritual map that encapsulates the entire corpus of human experience. They are not just poems of praise. Paul understood this, and under the inspiration of the Holy Spirit inserted a lament into a chapter that is about victory. He's able to claim victory precisely because he understands that lament is deeply woven into the path of victory.

Wright says, "We should not be surprised, then, that Paul finds in the Psalms both a map to see where he presently is (rejoicing in God's victory while still surrounded by persecution and danger of every kind) and a means by which he can bring both his celebrations and his sorrows into the personal presence of the God who searches the hearts."[4]

Paul is able to tell the Romans they are "more than conquerors" because, in Christianity, conquering is not the goal. Relationship is the goal. It was Caesar who called for conquest and domination, while Jesus shows mercy, lament, and forgiveness as the way of the Kingdom. This is why Paul can claim nothing can separate us from the love of God in Jesus Christ; "neither death nor life, nor angels nor rulers, nor things present nor things to come, nor powers, nor height nor depth, nor anything else in all creation." This leads us to a deeper understanding of true victory in the Christian faith. Lament is essential to this path of a full biblical faith, and its constant use perpetually reminds us that unless we learn to recover lament, we will also become people who do not walk in holistic victory.

Victory

Although victory has a wide diversity of expressions, often the only accepted form in the Church is praise and thanksgiving. While praise and thanking God for His victory is great, His triumph comes through His presence. Stated earlier, the victory of faith is "God with Us," Immanuel. Since the metanarrative of scripture mainly asks relational questions, we should understand victory and lament the same way.

Exploring the minor keys of life can be disorienting, but it's not without hope. God not only recognizes our darkness, He enters it and shines through it. Yet, when God enters our darkness, He's not aiming to elicit our praise, but to make us aware of the goodness of His presence. Even when He was on the Cross, Jesus didn't "praise" God in the way we normally consider praise, yet He remained faithful. God is with us in the middle of the darkness and the praise, the groans and the shouts of thanksgiving.

If Christianity is mainly about relationship with God, then self, others, and the rest of creation, seeing and resting in "God with Us" is the victory of lamenting faith. It is not only faithfulness when one is able to get to the point of thanksgiving and praise. It is the entire path, beginning-to-end.

Praise and Thanksgiving

Complaint finding its trust in God is ultimately hopeful, and that means it is not averse to praise and thanksgiving. Pemberton says: "Thanksgiving and lament not only grow from the same soil of faith but are part of the same organism. The practice of thanksgiving grows out of the prior practice of lament, so the loss of lament actually threatens a second type of faith talk: thanksgiving."[5] It is a paradox. Our violation must be taken seriously and never be seen to be good in itself. Recognizing the violation through vocalization sets the forms whereby the chaos can be brought into enough clarity that the light of the presence of "God with Us" presently gives victory. "God with Us" is our source for thankfulness, not the violation, *per se*. It is also this "with-ness" of God that produces the surprise of thanksgiving. Moltmann notes, "The man or woman who suffers God in the fellowship of the crucified Jesus can also praise God in the fellowship of the Jesus who is risen. The theology of the cross becomes the theology of doxology."[6]

Never Will I Leave You or Forsake You

God's presence is our ultimate victory, whether life remains dark or not. Walter Brueggemann brilliantly notes:

> The reason the darkness may be faced and lived in is that even in the darkness, there is One to address. The One to address is in the darkness but is not simply a part of the darkness (cf. John 1:1–5). Because this One has promised to be in the darkness with us, we find the darkness strangely transformed, not by the power of easy light, but by the power of relentless solidarity. Out of the "fear not" of that One spoken in the darkness, we are marvelously given new life, we know not how.[7]

Paul had a keen understanding that God never left or forsook him, even in incredibly difficult times. It is this type of intimate relationship with Jesus in both the good and the bad that gave him the confidence to tell the Philippian church,

> But whatever gain I had, I counted as loss for the sake of Christ. Indeed, I count everything as loss because of

> the surpassing worth of knowing Christ Jesus my Lord. For his sake I have suffered the loss of all things and count them as rubbish, in order that I may gain Christ and be found in him, not having a righteousness of my own that comes from the law, but that which comes through faith in Christ, the righteousness from God that depends on faith—that I may know him and the power of his resurrection, and may share his sufferings, becoming like him in his death, that by any means possible I may attain the resurrection from the dead.
>
> —Philip. 3:7–10

The Good News is ultimately relational, first with God and then with self, others, and the rest of creation. When one continually interacts with a faithful God who desires to be in communion with His children, even if the dialogue is filled with desperate cries and perceptions of betrayal, the victory of "God with Us" still holds. In this kind of safe relationship, lament is seen as a form of faith, not anti-faith.

We have covered a lot of biblical territory in this chapter. We have taken a look at lament in the life of Jesus, and in the life of Paul. What I've learned from each of these is that lament requires the courage to be honest, yet He always promises to be with us. Where our culture often tells us to suck it up and be happy, I see a different picture in the sweep of Scripture. The Bible itself gives us permission to lament and grieve our losses and pains in life. I did not understand this for a long time. Yet when I started to grasp that lament was a type of worship, it freed me from the tyranny of feeling like all I could ever do was praise God.

CHAPTER 7

Enemies and Allies of Forgiveness as Lament

In an age when many Christians think praise and thanksgiving are the only acceptable forms of worship, seeing forgiveness as a lament can be difficult. Several times, I've had people tell me to "just get over it." I have also heard the profoundly unfortunate idea that I would know when I'd truly forgiven because I wouldn't bring up the offense anymore. These types of harmful ideas produce all sorts of codependent and passive-aggressive behaviors, especially in the church. Although there are many enemies of forgiveness as lament, we'll focus on five.

Denial is the first enemy, and is foundational for all other enemies of lament. When a victim acts as if a violation is nonexistent or that no harm has been caused, denial finds a home. The ally of forgiveness as lament is acceptance, but not a fatalistic type of acceptance. Instead, we learn how to integrate a real violation into our lives as we recognize that we don't have to see life through the violation.

The second enemy of lament as forgiveness is violence as the answer to pain—violence expressed either towards self or others. The alternative to violence is "new possibility."

Third, we often want to remain in personal control when life feels out of control. Control is an enemy of forgiveness as lament because it puts self at the center of the narrative of life instead of God. In the process, people take on burdens no human can ultimately bear. Instead of pining for personal control, we're invited to see the compassion of God's sovereignty. God is not distant and aloof from our suffering.

Fourth, we'll explore the role of busyness as an enemy to lament. Busyness takes on many forms, but is undoubtedly an anesthetizing behavior that seeks to soothe pain through the medication of ignoring the violation through personal productivity. The ally of forgiveness as lament is sabbath. The recovery of sabbath provides space to complain and find trust in God by learning what the psalmist says in Psalm 46:10: "Cease striving and know that I am God."

Finally, we'll consider silence as an affront to the hope of forgiveness as lament. Victims must learn how to properly give voice to the ways in which they've been violated. Finding your voice can take many forms, yet none of them include silent resignation. The final ally of forgiveness as lament is vocalizing our violation.

Denial v. Acceptance

Denial can be understood as the foundational characteristic of each of the following enemies of lament. O'Connor says, "The first condition for healing is to bring the pain and suffering into view . . . Pain kept from speech, pushed underground and denied, will turn and twist and tunnel like a ferret until it grows in those lightless spaces into a violent, unrecognizable monster."[1] The path of denial is common, and can produce an immediate numbing effect as a coping mechanism. In many cases, numbing out is more bearable than facing the pain from the violation.

My personal choice for numbing out included alcohol and drug abuse. Some people choose the same things I did, while others numb themselves by being good people. They say what they think are the right things, they make their lives try to look perfect, yet all the while they numb themselves. The ways to numb ourselves are infinitely diverse.

Yet this form of denial has a dehumanizing effect on the one violated. To be fully human is to see violation for what it is and learn how to walk in the possibility of forgiveness. Yes, the refusal to numb out amidst pain is difficult, yet it is not impossible. Bessel van der Kolk wrote a brilliant book, *The Body Keeps the Score*, on how the entire body is influenced by traumas. His work covers physiology, psychology, and neurology in stunning fashion. Van der Kolk says,

> The essence of trauma is that it is overwhelming, unbelievable, and unbearable. Each patient demands that we suspend our sense of what is normal and accept that we are dealing with a dual reality: the reality of a relatively secure and predictable present that lives side by side with a ruinous, ever-present past."[2]

In order to see the possibility of not becoming what O'Connor warns about, a step forward is to see acceptance as an ally by means of which one can see forgiveness as lament. Tutu says, "We all experience pain. This is the inescapable part of being human. Hurt, insult, harm, and loss are inevitable aspects of our lives. Psychology calls it 'trauma,' and it often leaves deep scars on our souls. However, it is not the trauma itself that defines us. It is the meaning we make of our experiences that defines both who we are and who we ultimately become."[3]

Acceptance does not mean the violation is somehow good or all right. Instead, acceptance learns how to order the violated person's overall story. Living with acceptance in mind also means learning to accept the present; that not all our energies can go toward making sure another violation never happens again. It also involves accepting that reminders of past violation can't always be avoided.

In conclusion, the wise Desmond Tutu again continues his brilliance:

> We are harmed together, and we heal together. It is only in this fragile web of relationship that we rediscover our purpose, meaning, and joy after pain and loss . . . When we deny our feelings, when we choose not to name our hurts and instead reject the pain of our losses, we always end up seeking destruction . . . The only way to stop the pain is to accept it. The only way to accept it is to name it and, by naming it, to feel it fully. In so doing, you discover that your pain is part of the great, eternal tapestry of human loss and heartbreak. You realize you are not alone in your suffering, that

> others have experienced and survived what you have experienced, and that you too can survive and know joy and happiness again. When you embrace your feelings, you embrace yourself and allow others to embrace you too."[4]

The way of honest acceptance leads to the possibility of relating beyond our woundedness and gives space for the wound to become a scar. When this happens, we're empowered to heal in a way that is both true to the story of disunification and provides space for the possibility of reunification.

Violence v. New Possibility

The second enemy to lament is violence. Violence is a misplaced response when a violated person is unable or unwilling to be saddened and grieved by their violation. Sometimes this violence expresses itself in physical fighting and other times it can be vindictive words that try to cut others down. Furthermore, this type of violence does not only come out on others. Sometimes it is directed at ourselves, all the way from speaking harshly to yourself, to cutting, even to suicide.

Yet, there is a path forward that can provide an alternative to this violence. Lament, complaint that finds its trust in God, is this path. Lament produces the path of a new possibility of walking in forgiveness, which can result in reunification. Without complaining and finding trust in God after a violation, violent expression is natural. Brueggemann says:

> Sadness over loss that is unvoiced, unembraced, and unacknowledged a) turns to violence and b) precludes

> movement toward new possibility. Sadness unvoiced leads to violence, whether expressed in racial bigotry, hostility toward outsiders, readiness for attack on enemies, or self-hatred. Sadness unvoiced leads to a backward wish for recovery; as a result no energy is left for the pursuit or practice of new social possibility that lies beyond our old comfort zones.[5]

As Brueggemann says, if sadness can't find a voice through embracing and acknowledging violation, it will lead to violence. This is why the imprecatory psalms, such as Psalm 137, are helpful in voicing violations as an alternative to violence. In no way does God condone the murdering of the babies of enemies as is voiced in Psalm 137. Yet the alternative of carrying out such an atrocity is for a community to come together and vocalize what's in their hearts. This vocalization is treated both as confession, and the recognition for a faithful God to step in and speak healing into the great pains of violation. This alternative of lament allows for honest sadness and the beginning of a "new possibility" (as Brueggemann says) that gives space for grace-filled forgiveness.

The 20th-century poet Claude McKay wrote an insightful poem about racism called, "The White House." He doesn't hide from his own struggle not to hate, and recognizes that returning hate for hate perpetuates an endless cycle. His alternative is to embrace and voice his violation, which opens an opportunity to live a different narrative—a narrative filled with honesty and hope for change, even when the predatory society he sees perpetuated against African Americans is the White House itself.

"The White House"

Your door is shut against my tightened face,
And I am sharp as steel with discontent;
But I possess the courage and grace
To bear my anger proudly and unbent.
The pavement slabs burn loose beneath my feet,
A chafing savage, down the decent street;
And passion rends my vitals as I pass,
Where boldly shines your shuttered door of glass.
Oh, I must search for wisdom every hour,
Deep in my wrathful bosom sore and raw,
And find in it the superhuman power
To hold me to the letter of your law!
Oh, I must keep my heart inviolate
Against the potent poison of your hate.[6]

McKay uses profound language to describe the atrocity of racism. The door that gets "shut against his tightened face" shows a picture of hatred and deep anger. He remains proud and "unbent" in his opposition to deep injustice. McKay goes on to describe the disinterest of the President and lawmakers to enter into the pain of African Americans. Not only can those in the White House look out and see injustice, but their glass door "boldly shines" pridefully. McKay says it's impossible not to be wrathful and filled with hate. In fact, he needs "superhuman power" to withstand the "potent poison" of the President's hate.

This type of poetic and prophetic voice gives hope in the face of violence and oppression against African Americans. This poetic voice also gives a way for the possibility of walking in forgiveness, instead of living in violence toward enemies, just like Dr. Martin Luther King Jr. did.

Finally, when the violated come to a Triune God Who has been weeping over their violation, they find the strength to offer the gift of forgiveness to the violator. But never because they've learned to somehow downplay the violation. Rather, it's because they realize God has first allowed the violated at one time to be reunified with God. This in no way causes the violated not to call the violator to account. Instead, it offers the way of true forgiveness, which inherently means a violation has occurred and must be addressed.

Empowered by the Spirit, Christians have a new possibility for how to approach their violations. We can refuse to seek revenge for a wrong done and relinquish the desire for those who have offended us to pay us back personally. Instead, we desire to see reconciliation and restoration that are rooted in love. This is the way that violence does not have the last word, but also allows for the honesty of seeing forgiveness as a lament.

Control v. God's Sovereignty

The third enemy of lament is the desire to always be in control. Many believe Christian maturity means remaining silent, only speaking words of praise to God, or getting healed of the pain before ever vocalizing it to the community. This is all acceptable in modern-day Christian culture, yet none of these are mature, biblical responses. Many times, they can simply be expressions of the desire to remain in control.

When we learn God isn't disinterested in our plight, but suffers alongside humanity, then His sovereignty doesn't become a patronizing presence. Since God feels the pain of His children when they hurt, His control can lead to a deeper, hope-filled lament. When we feel the stranglehold of violation, we can turn to God with our complaint and say, "God, if You feel this pain more deeply than I do, then why do You keep doing this to Yourself! It doesn't make sense! You're in control of all things, and yet, we are both in a terrible situation!"

This sort of lament recognizes many different aspects of God's character. It recognizes first of all that his control is filled with mercy. He enters into the pain and offers healing from the inside out. Next, it testifies to the truth that God actually exists and is present. Third, this opens the conversation with God, whereby we're reminded of our own need for forgiveness. God has offered us forgiveness and we, in turn, learn to walk in forgiveness towards the one who violated us. Finally, when we learn to lament our own violation with our own need of forgiveness in view, something beautiful happens. It produces a joy that unshackles the violated person from being controlled by the wound. It also unshackles the one who caused the wound. It takes the devastation seriously, but doesn't allow devastation to have the final say.

Busyness v. Sabbath

The third enemy of forgiveness as lament is busyness. When we stay busy with work and our social lives, we can distract ourselves from pain. We can put on a front that makes it look like we've "gotten over" a violation. We Americans praise productivity, yet productivity meant to mask pain can leave a person empty in many ways, and gives sufferers a false sense of healing. Busyness may help us forget our violation and fill our wounded voids with accomplishment, but when we do this, we run the risk of wrongly believing we're only as good as what we do and produce. Our lives become based on a utilitarian end, instead of a relational one. In the process we become less human.

I did this for a long time. Since I have a relatively high capacity for long hours of work, I would spend twelve to fourteen hours a day working. Especially since much of this work happened in pastoral roles and through His Voice Global, many people would simply think I was a driven person who wanted to help others. Undoubtedly, this is part of it, but what I've grown to understand is that an inability to rest, always, literally always, holds a false view of self-importance up as a mirror.

Our culture of self-importance gives out accolades when those who have been harmed "rise above" the pain and suffering. We have this insatiable need to be bigger than what has happened to us. The pitfall is that we pine for identity and self-importance, instead of resting in the truth of grace, that we're already loved children of God.

Finally, busyness is an enemy of forgiveness as lament because it gives the impression that the violated person is still powerful. Now, the answer is not that the violated one is weak. The way forward is to rest not in our own power, but in the power of God. No longer do we have to conjure up the strength to show we remain in control and are powerful. Our life's narrative no longer has to focus on "having it together" in the face of violation. We can lay down our façade of strength and take on the hope of honesty in the midst of difficulty.

In order to combat busyness we must learn to recover the

need for Sabbath. The idea of Sabbath can be seen all the way back in the Creation narrative of Genesis 2:1–3:

> Thus the heavens and the earth were finished, and all the host of them. And on the seventh day God finished his work that he had done, and he rested on the seventh day from all his work that he had done. So God blessed the seventh day and made it holy, because on it God rested from all his work that he had done in creation.

The idea of rest is just as creative as the animal and plant kingdoms. It is something whereby humanity learns that a Sovereign God wants his image-bearers to see they are not "as good as what they do." Instead, Sabbath puts humanity in a position of seeing that God, the Provider, even allows Himself to rest, not because He is tired, but in order to set a pace whereby production is not the main narrative of the Metanarrative; instead, relationship is. This is why God goes on to give the fourth commandment, "Remember the Sabbath day, to keep it holy. Six days you shall labor, and do all your work, but the seventh day is a Sabbath to the LORD your God."

Within the rhythms of Sabbath, we learn to receive from God, as opposed to marching to the anthem of "doing." Sabbath informs the other six days of living, not the other way 'round. If this type of receiving were to be a focus of the Christian, then when a time of violation comes, the aim would not be to become busy in order to prove worth in the face of devastation, but instead would be to come to a tear-filled God who provides healing in dozens of different ways, yet does not allow a person to know they are only as good as their healing. They are a loved child of God, who graciously takes them into His arms during the time of violation. He gives the violated spaces to vocalize their pain, and then offers the healing balm of His presence as a way to provide the strength to walk in forgiveness towards the person who has caused so much pain.

It is this peace in God that provides a way for the violated to enter into the Triune community of God and receive healing that is provided by the One who stays in perfect communion at all times. God's tears empower the violated with the truth of their pain so that ultimately their violation will not be the predominant narrative of their lives. The Weeping Triune God gives the path of forgiveness as a gift that can be offered as a way to reunification, instead of the empty and stress-filled pursuit of busyness.

Silence v. Vocalizing

One of the greatest enemies of lament is continual silence. Many times people believe the lie that any negative or adverse thought towards a situation, God, or another person inherently indicate a lack of faith. This is not true. Ellington notes:

> Like a small child, lament keeps endlessly repeating "Mommy! Mommy! Mommy!" in that irritating tone of children that simply cannot be ignored. While lament may explore dark places and journey to extreme frontiers in a relationship with God, by its very nature it refuses to step back from that relationship into silence. The prayer of lament stakes all on the conviction that

> God hears and will answer. Ultimately, while the prayer of lament involves a degree of risk, to remain silent in the face of God's silence is to accept and embrace the certainty of hopelessness."[7]

Silent resignation must be seen as anathema in the Christian tradition; so must the thought that all negative thoughts lack faith. Brueggemann states:

> Serious religious use of the lament psalms has been minimal because we have believed that faith does not mean to acknowledge and embrace negativity. We have thought that acknowledgement of negativity was somehow an act of unfaith, as though the very speech about it conceded too much of God's "loss of control."[8]

Glenn Pemberton also gives brilliant insight as to the cost of silence:

> Silence in the place of difficult questions may come because we fear inappropriate, irreverent speech toward God. But silence may also be due to giving up on a relationship or because we have no real expectations of God. Oftentimes, we never ask God difficult questions because we are never disappointed or confused by God—and we are never disappointed because we never really expected God to do anything in the first place. No expectations, no disappointments, no questions for God: a low-risk, minimalist version of Christianity, safe from ever needing to have a difficult conversation

> with God. If we are to recover the voice of lament, we must dare to expect something from God—something that matters and something that will hurt us if God does not come through . . . My concern is that our loss of difficult questions for God is the result of our own apathy and the absence of a belief in a God who is at work in our lives and world.[9]

The ally of forgiveness as lament is choosing vocalization instead of silence. Yet vocalization is not simply words alone. Yes, words are helpful and forming, but they are not the only forms of vocalizing. Van der Kolk notes:

> We have learned that trauma is not just an event that took place sometime in the past; it is also the imprint left by that experience on mind, brain, and body. This imprint has ongoing consequences for how the human organism manages to survive in the present.
>
> Trauma results in a fundamental reorganization of the way mind and brain manage perceptions. It changes not only how we think and what we think about, but also our very capacity to think. We have discovered that helping victims of trauma find the words to describe what has happened to them is profoundly meaningful, but usually is not enough. The act of telling the story doesn't necessarily alter the automatic physical and hormonal responses of bodies that remain hypervigilant, prepared to be assaulted or violated at any time. For real change to take place, the body needs to learn that danger has passed and to live in the reality

> of the present. Our search to understand trauma has led us to think differently not only about the structure of the mind but also about the processes by which it heals.[10]

Undoubtedly, learning to form trauma into words, especially trauma that needs to offer forgiveness, is one of the ways in which healing can break in and help to order the devastation, yet it is not the only way to vocalize. One of the reasons for using poetry as a means for exploring forgiveness as a lament is because it is a genre that communicates much more beyond what is just printed. The structure, rhythm, and silence help to bring galvanizing clarity to the hope of seeing that vocalization provides a way forward. This is also why I use the Psalms and several other poems throughout this book.

In learning to express violation with and to the community through a wide array of vocalization, the path to healing and forgiving is made possible. It is in offering up the violation to the community that a unifying voice of empathy can also lead to the possibility of reunification with those who have been the violators. If the allies of acceptance, new possibility, God's sovereignty, Sabbath, and vocalizing will be adopted, then the enemies of denial, violence, control, busyness, and silence will be pushed out of the accepted ways of acting and living.

For me, this has included some intensive counseling, at times. It has meant that I have needed to learn how to actually take a day off and go on vacation. This has also meant that I have surrounded myself with incredibly godly people, over a wide range of ages, who speak candidly into my life.

As you explore various ways to express the allies that have been stated above, feel free to be creative. Sometimes what you do will work for a season, but then it will pass. Other times you will take on practices that will last a lifetime. Either way, know that God gives a wide array of ways to express the freedom of forgiveness being a lament. He is with you.

CHAPTER 8

A Way Forward

If we are to move into forgiveness of others who have caused us suffering, we must recognize that we're utterly dependent on God to do this work in us. Fortunately, we are not left alone in this. Within the intra-Trinitarian relationship, we see the most profound example of rejection—the Cross. As Father, Son and Holy Sprit lamented that atrocity, we too can learn how to root our own forgiveness in lament and see that relationship is ultimate, not violation. But to find a way forward, we must first recognize violation must be taken seriously and lamented. Otherwise, the path of forgiveness is a complete impossibility.

Violation is not ultimate, but the restored relationship in love is. As Moltmann says, "True human life comes from love, is alive in love, and through loving makes something living of other life too . . . How should we really get involved in this life, with its conflicts, pains, and disappointments, if we don't trust life more than death, and if we don't with every breath confess life, and stand up to the powers and conditions which disseminate death?"[1]

As C.S. Lewis aptly notes:

> Grief is like a long valley, a winding valley where any bend may reveal a totally new landscape . . . Sometimes the surprise is the opposite one; you are presented with exactly the same sort of country you thought you had left behind miles ago. That is when you wonder whether the valley isn't a circular trench. But it isn't. There are partial recurrences, but the sequence doesn't repeat.[2]

If Lewis is right that grief and lament are more like a winding valley than simply "getting over" something, we have to approach grief differently. Grief isn't about conquering a violation. Grief is meant to give voice to the violation and to find our ultimate victory in Emmanuel, "God with Us."

As van der Kolk says,

> Nobody can "treat" a war, or abuse, rape, molestation, or any other horrendous event, for that matter; what has happened cannot be undone. But what can be dealt with are the imprints of the trauma on body, mind, and soul: the crushing sensations in your chest that you may label as anxiety or depression; the fear of losing control; always being on alert for danger or rejection; the self-loathing; the nightmares and flashbacks; the fog that keeps you from staying on task and from engaging fully in what you are doing; being

unable to fully open your heart to another human being.[3]

Seeing forgiveness as a lament causes a deep empathy with great possibilities. First, it allows those in the present to learn from the past of those who have blazed a path of hope. Next, as we become more empathetic to the voices of the violated, it opens the door for people in the present to appropriate the lamenting voices of the oppressed. We learn how to see the diversity of biblical faith that produces a deeper and richer faith. As Moltmann says, "The more a person believes, the more deeply he experiences pain over the suffering in the world, and the more passionately he asks about God and the new creation."[4]

Third, in hearing the voices of those who have experienced personal violation, we begin to learn what it takes to live a lifestyle of *shalom*—holistic flourishing—that incorporates the violations into the entire narrative of life. It is a lifestyle that doesn't seek revenge for wrongs done. A lifestyle that relinquishes the desire for payback and seeks reconciliation and restoration rooted in love and the way of forgiveness. It is a stained-glass-window type of life.

Katherine Mansfield wrote the brilliant lament "To God the Father" after the death of her best friend, her brother. She could not come to terms with a God who claimed to be loving, yet allowed such a thing to happen. Mansfield's honest complaint to God helps others learn to entrust themselves to the God of grace Who helps carry their pain in the middle of personal violation.

"To God the Father"

To the little, pitiful God I make my prayer,
The God with the long grey beard
And flowing robe fastened with a hempen girdle
Who sits nodding and muttering on the all-too-big throne of Heaven.
What a long, long time, dear God, since you set the stars in their places,
Girded the earth with the sea, and invented the day and night.
And longer the time since you looked through the blue window of Heaven
To see your children at play in a garden . . .
Now we are all stronger than you and wiser and more arrogant,
In swift procession we pass you by.
"Who is that marionette nodding and muttering
On the all-too-big throne of Heaven?
Come down from your place, Grey Beard,
We have had enough of your play-acting!"
It is centuries since I believed in you,
But to-day my need of you has come back.
I want no rose-colored future,
No books of learning, no protestations and denials—
I am sick of this ugly scramble,
I am tired of being pulled about—
O God, I want to sit on your knees
On the all-too-big throne of Heaven,
And fall asleep with my hands tangled in your grey beard.[5]

This poem is a picture of a woman willing to wrestle with God like Jacob did in Genesis. Not all of her questions were answered, but she knew God was present and she was able to rest in Him: "On the all-too-big throne of Heaven / And fall asleep with my hands tangled in your grey beard." This is the same grey beard that was a picture of a distant, old God who did not care about her pain.

For one who is struggling with forgiveness, this type of lamenting prayer has the power to struggle with a seemingly distant God in a time of need. Instead of remaining bitter, there is a recognition that there is a different possibility of communion with a God Who breathes grace into the violation.

Walking with My Mom

As I said at the beginning of this book, I was able to be with my mom during her last week of life. My sister and I decided that I would talk to my mom about getting off of dialysis because her body was literally wasting away and the doctors said there was no hope for recovery. At the time of this conversation with my sister, I was in northern California at Scott River Lodge.

I fell asleep that night and had a vivid dream that my mom was in a paradise. She was wearing this exquisitely beautiful white dress (remember the vision of my mom playing in the yard as a child?). She looked at me with more clarity in her eyes than I had ever seen and she simply said, "There's no more stains!"

I woke up and cried with Amber. We packed and left for Michigan so I could talk with her and we could be together as a family.

When I arrived at the dialysis center, I sat down next to my mom and told her what the doctors had said. She stared back at me for a while, and then a stunning thing happened. She began confessing. She started talking about specific ways she had violated my sister and me, and she kept going on and on. I told her, "Mom, I forgive you." She continued to cry and confess and we wept together.

My sister, Phyllis, then came into the room. My mom held both our hands and started praying. Although she had prayed quite a bit in the past, we did not pray together often. She asked the Holy Spirit to be with her children six times in that prayer. As mom opened her eyes after the prayer, she simply said, "Wanna know what I'm thinking? That I have two great kids. That is what I am thinking."

She signed the papers to stop dialysis, and five days later she passed away, surrounded by her kids, grandkids, brother, and mom.

Conclusion

The goal of this book has been to articulate the Metanarrative, which is made up of three Acts: Unified, Disunified, and Reunified. As we explored the foundation and anatomy of lament in Scripture, we've proven that complaint that finds its trust in God is not only critical in worshipping God, but is also the foundation of learning how to live a lifestyle of forgiveness.

We came to understand violation, vocalization, and victory make up the anatomy of lament and forgiveness. And though not all lament is forgiveness, all forgiveness is filled with lament. Third, as we came to see forgiveness as lament, we made the case that God also forgives by lamenting. In the greatest point of all betrayal in history, the Cross, the Trinity responded in a symphonic, Triune lament. This enabled us to see the foundation of repentance, and forgiveness offers restoration and a way forward.

If sin is rooted in hiddenness, then faith finds its identity in honest togetherness. This means, in part, that praise to God isn't the only acceptable faith-filled expression. Lament has an intricate and valuable place. Forgiveness restores brokenness through lamenting the pain experienced by the violation of hiding and brings it to light through a restoring faith that believes in togetherness with God, self, others, and creation.

Restoration does not always look like smiles and hugs. Sometimes it has a disposition of tears and complaint that brings two parties together to restore broken communication and relationship. Forgiveness often looks like lament and produces a restoration big enough to be true to the pain of the offense, while also strong enough to come together and restore what was broken.

If a violated person refuses the response of violence towards self and others, a foundation of love has the opportunity to take its place. As we learn to rest in the graceful, yet tear-soaked, love of God, we learn how to love again. This love is essential, since Jesus says we must love our neighbors as ourselves. Restoration of relationship with those who have violated us is only part of God's work. Because God is a God of relational love, He reconciles us to Himself, to ourselves, and to one another.

Seeing the essential foundation of relational love is critical because relationship existed during the violation. But it was a relationship that was not healthy. The way of Jesus is to see that love is stronger than death and has power to repair that which was shattered. In the way of forgiveness, the desire is for relationship to be restored with love as its essence. This is the hope for forgiveness as lament.

The tears of God are the strength of history. Instead of the path of violence, one can learn how to take their tear-soaked violations to a loving and empathetic God. He is merciful and ever present. At the greatest affront in history—the

Cross—God stayed in perfect triune relationship through a symphonic, tear-soaked lament that had the fortitude to withstand violence. This was the way forward for mankind and forged the path of forgiveness to be a new anthem for reunification.

In the words of the brilliant Wiman, "There is some fury of clarity, some galvanizing combination of hope and lament, that is much needed now."[6] The key to seeing reunification and renewal of all four relationships of the Good News is the ingredient of tears that sets a solid, concrete foundation of hope. This reality of lament as the bedrock for understanding true forgiveness focuses on Jesus, the Cornerstone. And when we focus on Jesus in our lament, we know we can take our honest expressions of doubt and struggles, knowing it will be accepted as faith. Without lament, forgiveness ends up being patronizing. Violation must be taken seriously enough to vocalize, so that we can walk in humble victory with a God who feels the pain of all wounds. Lament is a jackhammer to denial, violence, and the desire to always to be in control and to stay busy. Without the hope of lament crushing these enemies, disunity and chaos end up lurking under the surface and pouncing in devastating proportions because they were never rooted out.

My prayer is that the Christian community will recover the path of lament as a viable form of worship. May our Christian communites learn to be safe places where we refuse trite platitudes and trival answers to the unspeakable horrors many of us face. May we be a people who abide in Immanuel, God with Us. If Jesus wept and entrusted His complaints to the Father, so should the rest of humanity. In the end, it is God's healing touch of gently wiping our tears away that allows for our wounds to be turned to scars. We lay down our need for revenge for the wrongs done against us and we relinquish our desire for our offenders to pay us back personally. To see reconciliation and restoration between violator and the violated, the one wronged must come to the Triune God in prayer to be reminded that, at one time, the one who is now violated was the violator.

As we remember God's tender reunification through forgiveness, the violated one can turn to the violator and offer, as a grace gift, the same forgiveness they have received. As Paul so poignantly notes in Romans 5:10–11, "For if while we were enemies we were reconciled to God by the death of his Son, much more, now that we are reconciled, shall we be saved by his life. More than that, we also rejoice in God through our Lord Jesus Christ, through whom we have now received reconciliation."

In the words of Moltmann,

> The fellowship of the God who is love has these two sides: it leads us into God's sufferings and into his infinite sorrow; but it will only be consummated in the feast of God's eternal joy and in the dance of those who have been redeemed from sorrow. For true love bears all things, endures all things and hopes all things in order to make the other happy, and thereby to find bliss itself.[7]

Psalm 23:6 says, "Surely goodness and mercy shall follow me all the days of my life, and I shall dwell in the house of the Lord forever." The dual reality of goodness and mercy is essential. The word "follow" in this passage paints a portrait of "hunting." It is the idea of goodness and mercy hunting one down. The hope comes when humanity sees that, by grace, God is actively hunting down His children with goodness. He does this by entering into their pain and offering healing from the inside out. He is a God who is not only concerned with praise, but He empowers His children to be agents of reunification as well.

God pursued humanity with goodness and mercy first, and this foundation will also provide us confidence that the lifestyle of complaining and finding trust in God, the way of lament, is also the path of faith that is filled with honesty, healing, and hope.

When I reflect on my own life growing up and the pain I endured, I wish those things had never happened. Yet what I continue to learn is there is hope in the midst of darkness. Lament and forgiveness go hand-in-hand. Both are hard and exhausting at times, but I've come to realize they are a great gift. My sincere hope is that you, the reader, can find hope in lament in light of the ways you have been harmed. Maybe you do not have the type of story I do, and maybe restoration with your violator will never happen. Maybe your life has been much more difficult than mine. I am not attempting to "compare stories" in any way. Your story is sacred, and so is mine. To be human is to live in a broken world marred by sin. We will sin against each other and others will sin against us. It hurts. Instead of minimizing our pain, instead of stuffing it way down inside, maybe we can learn the biblical art of lament again.

Learning the way of forgiveness as a form of lament offers the way for one to be "imprisoned to hope" (Zech. 9:12). It is an imprisonment to the wide terrain of salvation, which allows for one to walk humbly in the confidence of lament. The weak become strong, the broken are restored, and the violated learn to rest in victory. It is the honesty of forgiveness as lament that wins, reunites, and gives a way to see the Suffering God tenderly offering love. All is grace. May this poem be an honest expression of the hope-filled paradox that happens when lament becomes an expression of faithful worship and a foundational path to forgiveness.

Ecology of the Interior

Wilderness terrain
of the soul; diverse, pristine.
Dark and light mingle.

Ever flowing force,
rushing river breathes essence
perpetually.

The clapping glamor
of aspens anchored below
by roots entangled.

Black birds fly with the
wind gracefully propping their
pattern with beauty.

Mountain peaks tower
with white purity, holding
her varied landscape.

Waterfalls plunge down
poetically filling
vast arrays of life.

Forest variance:
Exquisite glow illumines
the soul's tapestry.

Notes

Introduction

1. T.S. Eliot, "Little Gidding," in *Four Quartets* (New York: Houghton Mifflin, 1943), 59.

Chapter 1: The Grand Story

1. Thomas McCall, *Forsaken* (Downers Grove: InterVarsity Press, 2012), 59.
2. This story will be explored in more depth in the section "Reunified."
3. Craig G. Bartholomew and Michael W. Goheen, *The Drama Of Scripture* (Grand Rapids: Baker Publishing, 2004), 129.

Chapter 2: The Foundation and Anatomy of Lament

1. Patrick D. Miller, "Heaven's Prisoners: The Lament as Christian Prayer," in *Lament: Reclaiming Practices in Pulpit, Pew, and Public Square* (Louisville: Westminster John Knox Press, 2005), 16.
2. Kathleen M. O'Connor, *Lamentations and the Tears of the World* (Maryknoll: Orbis Books, 2002), 9.
3. L. Gregory Jones, *Embodying Forgiveness: A Theological Analysis* (Grand Rapids: Eerdmans Publishing, 1995), 61.
4. Christian Wiman, *My Bright Abyss* (New York: Farrar, Straus and Giroux, 2013), 53.
5. Scott A. Ellington, *Risking Truth* (Eugene: Pickwick Publishing, 2008), 7.
6. Glenn Pemberton, *Hurting with God* (Abilene: Abilene Christian University Press, 2012), 48.
7. Ibid., 4.
8. Ellington, 13.
9. Ibid., 46.
10. Richard K. Fenn, "Ezra's Lament: The Anatomy of Grief," in *Lament: Reclaiming Practices in Pulpit, Pew, and Public Square* (Louisville: Westminster John Knox Press, 2005), 139.
11. Edward Hirsch, *How to Read a Poem* (Orlando: Harcourt, Inc., 1999), 80.

Chapter 3: Lament in the Old Testament Psalms

1. N.T. Wright, *The Case for the Psalms* (New York: HarperCollins Publishing, 2013), 5.
2. Pemberton, 75.
3. Wright, 72–73.
4. Walter Brueggemann, *The Message of the Psalms* (Minneapolis: Augsburg Publishing House, 1984), 77.
5. Charles L. Bartow, "Till God Speaks Light: Devotional Reflections on Lamentation with Verse," in *Lament: Reclaiming Practices in Pulpit, Pew, and Public Square* (Louisville: Westminster John Knox Press, 2005), 163–64.

Chapter 4: Forgiveness as Lament For Humanity

1. Lewis Smedes, *The Art of Forgiving* (New York: Ballantine Books, 1996), 7–8.
2. Ibid., 56–57.
3. Although this present book does not have the space to explore an in-depth theodicy, it seems the biggest problem of evil is that, in view of God feeling the pain of His children even more deeply than they do, why does He keep allowing this to happen to Himself? This question is a deep mystery, but one that opens the door for seeing a God who is not distant, but is in the midst of suffering and is fully focused on being reunified, through the solidarity of tear-soaked lament, with His people, by offering forgiveness.

4. Brian Zahnd, *Radical Forgiveness* (Lake Mary: Passion, 2013), 13.
5. Jones, 47.
6. Ibid., 66–67.
7. Ibid., xii.
8. Martin Luther King Jr., *Strength to Love* (Minneapolis: Fortress Press, 2010), 45.
9. Desmond Tutu and Mpho Tutu, *The Book of Forgiving* (New York: Harper One, 2014), 96–97.
10. Miroslav Volf, *Exclusion and Embrace* (Nashville: Abingdon Press, 1996), 124.
11. Ellington, 27.
12. O'Connor, 102.
13. Miroslav Volf, *Free of Charge* (Grand Rapids: Zondervan, 2005), 129.
14. Jones, 4.
15. Ibid., 15.
16. This quote is from an unpublished commentary on the book of Matthew by Dr. Rodney Reeves.
17. Volf, 131.
18. Jones, 6.
19. King, 45.

Chapter 5: A God Who Forgives by Lamenting

1. William Stacy Johnson, "Jesus' Cry, God's Cry, and Ours," in *Lament: Reclaiming Practices in Pulpit, Pew, and Public Square* (Louisville: Westminster John Knox Press, 2005), 80.
2. McCall, 27.
3. Ibid., 46.
4. Robert C. Dykstra, "Rending the Curtain: Lament as an Act of Vulnerable Aggression," in *Lament: Reclaiming Practices in Pulpit, Pew, and Public Square* (Louisville: Westminster John Knox Press, 2005), 60.
5. Jurgen Moltmann, *The Crucified God* (Minneapolis: First Fortress Press, 1993), 46–47.
6. Ibid., 47.
7. First with God, then self, then others, and the rest of creation.
8. Moltmann, 153.
9. Walter Brueggemann, *The Prophetic Imagination* (Minneapolis: Augsburg Press, 2001), 56.
10. Wiman, 25.
11. Nicholas Wolterstorff, *Lament for a Son* (Grand Rapids: Eerdmans Publishing, 1987), 90.
12. McCall, 91.

Chapter 6: Lament in the New Testament

1. Miller, 21.
2. Nancy Guthrie, *Hearing Jesus Speak into Our Sorrow* (Carol Stream: Tyndale House, 2009), 7.
3. Ibid., xx.
4. Wright, 114–15.
5. Pemberton, 26.
6. Jurgen Moltmann, *The Trinity and the Kingdom* (Minneapolis: Augsburg Fortress Publishing, 1993), 8.
7. Brueggemann, *The Message of the Psalms*, 12.

Chapter 7: Enemies and Allies of Forgiveness as Lament

1. O'Connor, 95.
2. Bessel van der Kolk, *The Body Keeps the Score* (New York: Viking Penguin, 2014), 195.
3. Tutu and Tutu, 70.
4. Tutu and Tutu, 104–05.
5. Walter Brueggemann, *Reality, Grief, Hope* (Grand Rapids: Eerdmans Publishing, 2014), 82.
6. Claude McKay, "The White House," in *American Negro Poetry* (New York: Hill and Wang, 1974), 31–32.
7. Ellington, 4.
8. Brueggemann, *The Message of the Psalms*, 52.

9. Pemberton, 172–73.
10. Van der Kolk, 21.

Chapter 8: A Way Forward

1. Jurgen Moltmann, *The Coming of God* (Minneapolis: Augsburg Fortress Press, 2004), 53–54.
2. C.S. Lewis, *A Grief Observed* (New York: HarperOne, 1996), 60.
3. Van der Kolk, 203.
4. Moltmann, *The Trinity and the Kingdom*, 49.
5. Katherine Mansfield, "To God the Father," in *The 20th Century in Poetry* (New York: Pegasus Books, 2013), 72.
6. Wiman, 52.
7. Moltmann, *The Trinity and the Kingdom*, 42.

Bibliography

Bartholomew, Craig G. and Michael W. Goheen. *The Drama of Scripture.* Grand Rapids: Baker Publishing, 2004.

Bartow, Charles L. "Till God Speaks Light: Devotional Reflections on Lamentation with Verse." *Lament: Reclaiming Practices in Pulpit, Pew, and Public Square* Louisville: Westminster John Knox Press, 2005.

Brueggemann, Walter. *The Message of the Psalms.* Minneapolis: Augsburg Publishing House, 1984.

---. *The Prophetic Imagination.* Minneapolis: Augsburg Fortress, 2001.

---. *Reality, Grief, Hope.* Grand Rapids: William B. Eerdmans Publishing Company, 2014.

Dykstra, Robert C. "Rending the Curtain: Lament as an Act of Vulnerable Aggression." *Lament: Reclaiming Practices in Pulpit, Pew, and Public Square.* Louisville: Westminster John Knox Press, 2005.

Eliot, T.S. *Four Quartets.* New York: Houghton Mifflin Harcourt Publishing Company, 1943.

Ellington, Scott A. *Risking Truth.* Eugene: Pickwick Publications, 2008.

Fenn, Richard K. "*Ezra's* Lament: The Anatomy of Grief." *Lament: Reclaiming Practices in Pulpit, Pew, and Public Square.* Louisville: Westminster John Knox Press, 2005.

Guthrie, Nancy. *Hearing Jesus Speak into Our Sorrow.* Carol Stream: Tyndale House Inc., 2009.

Hirsch, Edward. *How to Read a Poem.* 1st ed. Orlando: Harcourt, Inc., 1999.

Johnson,William Stacy. "Jesus' Cry, God's Cry, and Ours." *Lament: Reclaiming Practices in Pulpit, Pew, and Public Square.* Louisville: Westminster John Knox Press, 2005.

Jones, L. Gregory. *Embodying Forgiveness.* Grand Rapids: Wm. B. Eerdmans Publishing Co., 1995.

King, Martin Luther, Jr. *Strength to Love.* Minneapolis: Fortress Press, 2010.

Lewis, C.S. *A Grief Observed.* New York: HarperOne, 1996.

Mansfield, Katherine. "To God the Father." *The 20th Century In Poetry.* New York: Pegasus Books LLC., 2013.

McCall, Thomas. *Forsaken.* Downers Grove: InterVarsity Press, 2012.

McKay, Claude. "The White House." *American Negro Poetry.* New York: Hill and Wang, 1974.

Miller, Patrick D. "Heaven's Prisoners: The Lament as Christian Prayer." *Lament: Reclaiming Practices in Pulpit, Pew, and Public Square.* Louisville: Westminster John Knox Press, 2005.

Moltmann, Jurgen. *The Coming of God.* Minneapolis: Fortress Press, 2004.

---. *The Crucified God.* Minneapolis: First Fortress Press, 1993.

---. *The Trinity and the Kingdom.* Minneapolis: Augsburg Fortress Publishers, 1993.

O'Connor, Kathleen M. *Lamentations and the Tears of the World.* Maryknoll: Orbis Books, 2002.

Pemberton, Glenn. *Hurting with God.* Abilene: Abilene Christian University Press, 2012.

Smedes, Lewis. *The Art of Forgiving.* New York: Ballatine Books, 1996.

Tutu, Desmond, and Mpho Tutu. *The Book of Forgiving.* New York: Harper One, 2014.

Van der Kolk, Bessel. *The Body Keeps the Score.* New York: Viking Penguin, 2014.

Volf, Miraslov. *Free of Charge.* Grand Rapids: Zondervan Publishing, 2005.

Wiman, Christian. *My Bright Abyss.* New York: Farrar, Straus and Giroux, 2013.

Wolterstorff, Nicholas. (1987) *Lament for a Son.* Grand Rapids: Wm. B. Eerdmans Publishing Co., 1987.

Wright, N.T. (2013) *The Case for the Psalms.* New York: HarperCollins Publishers, 2013.

Zahnd, Brian. *Radical Forgiveness.* Lake Mary: Passion, 2013.

Acknowledgments

Thank you to the His Voice Global team: Mark and Roc'c, Bruce, Danielle, Justin and Allison, Darrell, Stan, and Amber—you guys are a profound gift to me and this book. HVG would not exist without you.

Sis, you taught me what it was to see Jesus when the last thing I knew was my need for Him. You are one of the smartest people I know. Your life of love and grace is a gift to see.

Robync, Katie, and Allison, I love you and am beyond grateful. You are beautiful and amazing.

Many people over the years have helped to shape me. James Crabtree, your constant humor and deep thinking are a great encouragement to me. Bill and Jane Thomas, you have been exquisite friends and faithful people to breathe life into us. "The Prophetic Rancher," Larry Stewart, your life and generosity have shown me grace in ways I had never known. Rodney Reeves, your life has taught me more than you will ever know. Matt Chandler, Josh Patterson, and Michael Bleeker, your humility and tenacity is something I admire deeply. Steve Knox, you have helped me to see a better picture of life than anyone else I have been around. Kevin Kahlden, your constant friendship is stunning. Tyndall Wakeham, you continually show me how to think deeply, love deeper, and live with hope. Ian and Melissa Christopher, your presence in my life is a picture of God's abundant love. Jerrell and Kay Altic, your continual pursuing care and kindness is profound. Tedashii Anderson, your constant friendship and kind witness have taught me much. John Durham, I have said it to dozens of people: you are the greatest pastor I know. Brian Zahnd, thank you for continually provoking me into a deeper relationship with Jesus. Adam Thomason, your prophetic voice has helped to continually orient me, especially when the times have been filled with storms. Mike Goeke, your life of authenticity and compassion has taught me more about these realities of God than any other person I know.

My editor, Matt Johnson: seeing you take a PhD dissertation and turning it into a book that is half the length, while trying to work out some of the "academic-ese" and adding some of my personal story has been a blast to watch. You are intensely gifted.

Amber, you are my best friend and perpetual source of joy and hope. Through the tears and smiles, you are always present. Titus, I love your mind and your mercy. Justus, you are brilliant and joyful. All three of you have taught me God's faithfulness. What a team!

Finally, thank you, Father, Jesus, and Holy Spirit. Your fellowship, love, mercy, grace, and encouragement mean more than any words can be written.

His Voice Global partners with local communities to raise up leaders. They are committed to orphans and vulnerable children, widows, and church leadership to see relationships restored and communities renewed.

Through collaboration with their indigenous partners, they help to provide a circle of care, theological training, and economic development within the community. Currently they have partnerships in South Sudan, Kenya, and India.

All profits from *Imprisoned to Hope* will be donated to His Voice Global.

www.HisVoiceGlobal.com

www.ingramcontent.com/pod-product-compliance
Lightning Source LLC
Chambersburg PA
CBHW030838090426
42737CB00009B/1018

* 9 7 8 1 6 3 2 9 6 1 3 1 0 *